Vygotsky, Education & Revolution

Vygotsky, Education & Revolution

Shirley Franklin

Vygotsky, Education & Revolution
by Shirley Franklin

First edition published by Bookmarks in 2021

© Bookmarks Publications Ltd
c/o 1 Bloomsbury Street, London WC1B 3QE
www.bookmarksbookshop.co.uk

ISBN 978-1-912926-84-8 paperback
ISBN 978-1-912926-85-5 Kindle
ISBN 978-1-912926-86-2 epub
ISBN 978-1-912926-87-9 pdf

Typeset by Bookmarks Publications
Cover design by Ben Windsor
Printed by Halstan & Co Ltd,
Amersham, Buckinghamshire, England

Contents

About the Author

Shirley Franklin taught students with Special Educational Needs in London comprehensive schools for 25 years. She then taught Education Studies and on teacher training courses for twenty years at Middlesex University, the Institute of Education and at what is now the University of Lancaster.

She has written academic articles on Vygotsky and on teaching and learning and has published teaching materials.

Since 2010 she has been a health campaigner. She has been a member of the Socialist Workers Party since 1979.

Acknowledgments

I am particularly grateful to Tony Burgess and Jane Miller who introduced me to Vygotsky's theories on their English Language and Literature MA programme at the Institute of Education. My friend and colleague, Jan Derry, shared many a glass of wine exchanging thoughts and ideas about his work, helping to extend and deepen my understanding. Love and appreciation are due to her too.

A team of people helped in the final production of this book. John Parrington, Jane Bassett, Shaun Doherty and Dave Gilchrist read early drafts, offering valuable comments and advice. Thanks to Sandra Shepherd for the proofreading and to Ben Windsor for the imaginative cover design and to Colm Bryce who provided on-going support and guidance throughout the whole publishing process.

Finally love and thanks to my sons, Joe and Jethro, for their advice, support and exchange of ideas.

Introduction

Lev Semyonovich Vygotsky was a Russian Marxist Jewish educational philosopher and psychologist who was born in 1896, before the first Revolution of 1905, and died of tuberculosis in the midst of Stalin's repressive regime in 1934. Despite recurrent bouts of illness, during this short period of his life he was exceptionally productive in his research, practice and writings.

His short life gives a fascinating glimpse of the dynamism of ideas and activity that flourished through the 1917 October Revolution in Russia. The lives of Jews like Vygotsky were transformed from dreadful oppression under Tsarist rule to liberation. But then we see the crushing impact of Stalinism on intellectual and creative endeavours in the 1930s. This chapter gives a broad outline of his life and of his ideas about children's development.[1]

Vygotsky played various important roles for the Russian government following the 1917 Revolution, advising and representing it, in the broad field of education. He was a polymath: as well as being an exceptional linguist, he was a literary expert, psychiatrist, psychologist and philosopher. Despite his tragically early death, aged 37, he left hundreds of articles, mainly taken from his lectures, three published books and detailed notes recently published in *Vygotsky's Notebooks*.[2] These writings portray his commitment to the development of a Marxist psychology, a materialist, historical and social interpretation of how we develop, think, learn, feel and behave.

He was a practitioner, as a teacher trainer and later as a psychologist working with children with a range of mental health challenges or special needs, and with adults, diagnosed with schizophrenia and Alzheimer's Disease. There is little known of his case work. Most of what we know are his academic ideas. He lectured and wrote about psychology, special needs and schooling in revolutionary and post-revolutionary Russia in the 1920s and 1930s. His findings and style are extraordinarily relevant today, as testing dominates education, enforced by governments demanding higher standards from schools and teachers, but who have little understanding of how children learn. Today's education system demands that learning is seen in terms of styles, skills and tests. Vygotsky shows us that learning is a more complex process: it is social, interactive, cultural; it is a developmental process and takes place in a specific context. We filter what we think and learn through the medium of language or other signs and tools—so our learning is "mediated".

Vygotsky is now known in educational circles for his psychological and pedagogical theories about the *zone of proximal development,* developmental learning and learning through activity.[3] The many papers that he wrote were informed by observations of his patients, from his research and his theoretical analysis. His most renowned works are *Thought and Language* and *Mind in Society*, the latter being a collection of papers published in the West in 1978, 44 years after his early death. We are fortunate that his original notebooks have recently been collated by Zavershneva and Van der Veer, providing a fascinating insight into the formulation of his ideas.[4]

He became a revolutionary Marxist during the October Revolution of 1917. Despite being frequently cited in academic circles, it is not so well known, nor understood, that his educational and psychological theories are based on his commitment to a theory rooted in Marxism, that his political, educational and psychological theories interrelate and that he played a significant role in the development of education and psychology in revolutionary Russia, in theory and in practice.

His two well-known texts were translated at a time when Marxism in the West was often perceived as equivalent to Stalinism and many of his political references and the language he used were conveniently adapted to fit the Cold War period. The first edition of *Thought and Language*, which was published in the West in 1962, omitted all his references to Lenin, and many referring to Marx and Engels. Much of Vygotsky's work was banned in his own country until after Stalin's death in 1953 for not being sufficiently Stalinist, and in capitalist America for being too Russian, and therefore associated with communism and revolution.[5] Furthermore, much of what he wrote has become distorted through the complexities of translation and through different historical knowledge frames of the period.[6]

Lev Vygotsky

At the young age of 37, Vygotsky died of tuberculosis, which had afflicted him for much of his adult life. But while he was being treated during long stays in clinics, he developed the basis of many of his seminal theories, most of which were driven and infused by his new-found Marxism. Like many other theoreticians, his ideas changed and developed over the 20 years of his writings.

Vygotsky's short life gives a fascinating glimpse of the dynamism of ideas and activity that flourished after the 1917 October Revolution in Russia. The lives of Jews like Vygotsky were transformed from dreadful oppression under Tsarist Russia to liberation after the Revolution. But the 1930s saw the crushing impact of Stalinism on intellectual and creative endeavours.

This book is an attempt to show the background and development of his ideas, and to explain them accessibly for students, teachers, parents and others who are interested in language, communication, special educational needs, thought, development of the individual, learning and their inter-relationship with the individual and the culture and society in which that individual interacts. I hope this will throw more light on how we, and our children, think, learn and develop. It should also help us to better understand our world through a Marxist lens.

The next two chapters trace the story of his life. In the fourth chapter there is an analysis of how Vygotsky developed a Marxist psychology. The following chapters look at Vygotsky's theories of language and learning, including the *zone of proximal development*, special educational needs, play and finally his legacy.

Chapter 1
Early Life

Vygotsky was born in 1896 into a close, intellectual, middle-class Jewish family in Tsarist Russia, which had a profound impact on his identity and his theories. Russia, at this time, was abounding with high culture and industrialisation on the one hand, and suffering from brutal repression on the other, particularly against the substantial Jewish population.

The family lived in a large flat in Gomel (close to Chernobyl, in what is now Belarus), when the Jewish population of over 20,000 was more than 50 percent of the total population of the town. This number rose to over 40,000 by 1939, nearly 30 percent of the population. But in 1941 Nazi Germany occupied the area, by which time many of the Jewish inhabitants had fled. The rest were put into three ghettos.

The discrimination against Jews in Tsarist Russia meant that they were only allowed to live in specified areas and only attend Jewish schools. Local Jewish children attended Jewish religious primary schools. There were two secondary schools, known as gymnasiums—one was a private boys' school, the other was a government school. In the 1920s, after the 1917 Revolution, there was a Jewish teacher training college in Gomel.

Antisemitism was opposed by the many different Jewish religious and political groups in Gomel—Zionist Socialists, the Bund—a Jewish Marxist Social Democratic group, committed to the revolutionary movement in Russia, active against state-organised terror of Jews, a deeply orthodox group called

Liubavich Hasidim, and the Association for the Enlightenment of the Jews of Russia (OPE).[7]

In 1903, when he was seven years old, soon after he and his family moved to Gomel, there was a pogrom there, in which ten Jews were murdered, many were wounded and many had their property looted. The Bund organised resistance to this state-organised terror. The members involved were put on trial and most were acquitted. In a three-day pogrom three years later, houses were burnt down.[8]

Vygotsky grew up in a middle-class orthodox household in which his father Semyon, a successful banker, was also politically active. Semyon was an active member of the local Bund and acted as a witness at the above trial of Bund members, citing the increased awareness of Gomel Jews of their lack of human rights, which created tensions. He was also leader of the local OPE, whose motto was "Be a man in the street and a Jew at home".[9] He had a well-stocked library in his home and was the founder of a local public library that was housed below the Vygotsky residence. Their home was also the headquarters of the Jewish Colonialisation Association (JCA), a charitable group that supported the emigration of Jews from Russia to less discriminatory countries.

Semyon introduced Vygotsky to a wide range of literature and philosophy, particularly Hegel and Spinoza, instigating in him a lifelong interest. Vygotsky, his family and friends were involved in a variety of cultural events around the library, which was also used by the non-Jewish local population.[10]

Vygotsky's mother, Celia Moiseyevna Vygodskaya, was a trained teacher and, like her husband, was also fluent in a variety of languages but never actually taught, since she was looking after and educating the children.

The family spoke Yiddish and could read Hebrew; they read the Bible and kept the Jewish festivals. On 5 November 1909 Vygotsky, aged 13, had his barmitzvah and in his late teens wrote extensively about Jewish issues. He was educated at home for five years and was then enrolled for two years in a private Jewish secondary school. He was a successful student, particularly in history, maths, literature and philology, a form of socio-historical linguistics. He also enjoyed swimming, a wide range of reading, stamp-collecting, chess, writing to pen-pals in Esperanto, as well as the society of his friends, with whom he discussed Hegel's philosophy of history and poetry. He and his school friends collaborated with their homework, with him helping them with complex school topics.

This segregation had an impact on Vygotsky's education. He left school in 1913, with a gold medal in recognition of his academic achievement and, following the advice of his parents, chose to study medicine.

His *Notebooks* show that during his early student years, from 1915 to 1917, Vygotsky was involved in Jewish political and philosophical issues. He was deeply concerned about antisemitism and his writings showed how he considered that, despite the activity of the Bund, on the whole the majority of the local Jewish population were far too indifferent and passive in their opposition to their oppression through restrictive laws and humiliation. He wrote on March 1917: "Deep decadence through which the Jews are going must be replaced by a renaissance of the people's consciousness: only then shall the people's will come alive".[11]

This notion of the importance of Jewish consciousness, and identity, led him to reject Zionism as a solution to antisemitisim, despite the involvement of this father in helping Jews to escape to other countries. At the time, Vygotsky thought that Jews carry their oppression wherever they go. That oppression would not be resolved by going to Palestine. In 1917, in his *Notebooks* he wrote:

> The 'prophecy' of Zionism is wrong. Not only will we not go to Palestine, we have not even completed the golus.[12] It is still going on. Disintegration is what threatens the Jews, and not assimilation, not destruction.[13]

Vygotsky's zeal about Judaism was completely replaced during 1917-18, when the powerful impact of the October Revolution and Karl Marx's politics became his source of inspiration. However, Vygotsky retained his Jewish identity.

Despite the restrictions placed on Jews going to universities, he was fortunately one of the three percent of Jews permitted, through a draw, to study at the University of Moscow, Russia's oldest university. Vygotsky did not enjoy his medical course and after a month, he transferred to law.[14] While studying for his law degree from 1913 to 1917, he also enrolled as a student in psychology, linguistics, history and philosophy at the progressive and free Shaniavsky People's University, an unofficial university founded by anti-Tsarist Marxists, and whose lecturers were considered to be inspirational teachers, respected scholars and scientists. He studied a linguistic course entitled 'The Internal Form of the Word", as well as reading the international research of psychologists such as the American William James (1842-1910), whose work analysed religion.

He wrote: "...while still at the university, I started a study of psychology and continued through all subsequent years. Since then I did not interrupt my studies in this field".[15]

These studies at the Shaniavsky University provided him with politically-imbued knowledge that impacted on his work for the rest of his life.

He graduated from both universities in 1917, the year of Russia's February and October Revolutions. Culture, in terms of theatre, literature, poetry, art and music, flourished in the revolutionary fervour immediately following 1917. Vygotsky was an active and informed participant in some of these cultural events, working as a local cultural official in Gomel between 1921 and 1923. He visited the theatre regularly with his sister and reviewed performances. An interpretation of Hamlet that he saw at this time had a lasting impact. At 19 years old he wrote an analysis of the play, which became the subject of his thesis for the Shaniavsky University, as well as a public lecture several years later, and the chapter of his first book *The Psychology of*

Art in 1925. He also wrote an analysis of Dostoevsky's writing, to whom he referred, along with other Russian dramatists and novelists, in his psychological works. This expertise and passion for literature is shown in many of his writings, which are peppered with literary examples and references.

Vygotsky with his students in 1929

The discrimination against the Jewish population had meant that Jews were banned from many jobs, teaching being one of them. However, life for Jews improved after the Revolution. When Russia regained control of Gomel from Germany in 1919, the previous restrictions were lifted and Vygotsky was able to start teaching literature, aesthetics, philosophy and Russian language in a vocational school, and psychology in the teachers' college. He set up a psychology laboratory for the study of children and adults with a variety of special needs and mental health problems. He also maintained his interest in the arts and education as Head of Art and Aesthetic Education in Gomel's Department of Education, through organising reading groups discussing novels and poetry and becoming involved in the running of the local theatre.

He was a popular teacher and lecturer and was nominated in the local newspaper as the best teacher in the Gomel province. The Pedagogical Council noted that he "showed pedagogical tact, eagerness, and erudition in this teaching...".[16] Many of the lectures that he delivered at Gomel's teaching training college between 1921 and 1923 are included in his second book, *Educational Psychology*, published in 1926. This publication includes many of the theories he was to develop in later years. It also shows his commitment to the development of an innovative education system in the new Russia. In the preface to this book, Vygotsky wrote of his intention that the book would play a role in the Soviet school of pedagogy, and of his wish to develop a pedagogy based on the developing science of psychology.

The trainee teachers whom he was addressing were the new generation of revolutionary Russian educators. This work broke with the then current authoritarian pedagogy by emphasising the importance in the educational learning *process* of the *collaborative role of the teacher with the child*, with the child's environment and with her experiences and motivations. He was not advocating an informal type of pedagogy, but one that was clearly structured, had goals, that was led by the teacher, and where there was a dynamic interaction between student and teacher.[17] It is a model that might be described in terms of *apprenticeship*.

His theoretical ideas on consciousness were to change quite radically in the next decade. In the early 1920s Vygotsky had been influenced by the reflexological, more physically-orientated theories of his compatriot, Pavlov. Pavlov focused on an analysis of behaviour in terms of the nervous system, which understood behaviour in terms of learned actions. We can see this influence in Vygotsky's early work, together with an understanding of the important role of language in thinking.

While Vygotsky was never a member of the Communist Party, he had become a Marxist revolutionary. Near the end of *Educational Psychology* he wrote: "The revolution undertakes the re-education of all mankind", a statement that seems to reflect Vygotsky's own political conversion, having become a Marxist during the October Revolution.[18] As Van der Veer and Valsiner comment, his reference to Trotsky's notion of the transformation of the individual through revolution has meant that this work was not re-issued under Stalin's rule in Russia.[19] To read this book in that country required a permit from the KGB which allowed the reader into the restricted room in the library. On the other hand, according to Van der Veer, Vygotsky never discussed class in his work for which some Marxists have criticised him.[20]

His psychological work was also developing: his laboratory experiments led to a report on *Methods of Reflexological and Psychological Investigation* which he presented in 1924 to the Second All-Russian Psycho-Neurological Congress (SPON) in Leningrad.[21] By this time he had formed a collaboration with Alexander Luria, who remembered that Vygotsky conducted these presentations with no notes, holding a blank piece of paper! This paper reflects the expanding impact of revolutionary ideas in psychology, where Vygotsky challenged prevailing Russian notions of stimulus-response theories as being inadequate scientific explanations for "particular and individual behaviours". Vygotsky pointed out that mind and behaviour are inseparable, and he criticised the behaviourists for having a dualist approach that separates the mind from actions. Vygotsky critiqued American behaviourist theory as insufficient for explaining individual differences in development. Consciousness was viewed by those behaviourists as being independent from behaviours, an erroneous conclusion, as Marx had pointed out in *The German Ideology*.[22] He incorporated a Gestalt approach, developed in Germany, which understands individual psychology in a holistic manner, including people's histories, as well as the symptoms displayed or perceptions described.

Vygotsky's lectures excited Marxist psychologists working in Moscow State University and he was invited to become a staff member of the Moscow Institute of Experimental Psychology as a senior scientific researcher. Luria was so impressed by his talk at the SPON conference that he and his colleague Leontiev decided to team up with Vygotsky, in what they called a "troika". Luria describes Vygotsky as being the "acknowledged leader". Their work focused on developing a new Marxist science that addressed human psychological processes. In the same year Vygotsky started to work in the Centre for Physically and Mentally Retarded Children at the

People's Commissariat of Education in Moscow, where he became Director of the Institute.

This collaboration with other psychologists, such as Luria and Leontiev, and with his students, was a pattern that he was to follow for the rest of his life. Joint exploration of ideas was a practice that he had experienced from childhood; it is in the Jewish tradition of the chavrusa, where Jewish students study the Bible in groups of two to five. Vygotsky saw collaboration, learning with another person, as an essential ingredient to successful learning. It underpins his theory of the *zone of proximal development*, to which he referred in *Thought and Language* and *Mind in Society*, and his commitment to apprenticeship as an effective means of learning.

Vygotsky with his daughter Gita

In 1924 Vygotsky married Roza Semkhova. His notes, written on his trip to London a year later, show his deep love for her. They had two daughters, one of whom, Gita, spent her life disseminating her father's ideas, and acting as curator for his many papers.

At this time, Vygotsky was developing his practical and academic work with children with disabilities, particularly in terms of the education and development of children. Many of his articles and lectures were published in the contemporary Soviet press, but several were unpublished. In 1926 he founded a laboratory for the study of *defectology* (the term applied to disability or special needs), which in 1929 became the Experimental Institute of Defectology. An early exponent of social inclusion of the "handicapped", he was adamant that the special schools should share the Soviet aims for all education—productive labour and self-sufficiency—so that the children in them enjoyed the benefits of a social education, and did not perceive themselves as different in a negative sense. Many of the papers that emerged from this research can be found in a collation of his work, *The Collected Works of L S Vygotsky, Volume 2, The Fundamentals of Defectology.*[23]

Like his contemporary educational psychologist, Jean Piaget, Vygotsky tried out some of his ideas about children's cognitive development on his daughters but then moved onto mass studies with children and adults.

In his short life, despite his knowledge of a range of international theories, Vygotsky only travelled abroad once. This was in his role as Director of Education of Children with Defects, under the people's Commissariat of Education, Russia and Socialist Federative Soviet Republic, and as a Lecturer at the Second Moscow State University. He travelled to London in June 1925, where he presented a paper on *Principles of Social Education for Deaf and Dumb Children in Russia.*[24]

The notes he wrote on this trip, reproduced in the *Notebooks*, show that he missed Roza dreadfully and that he found the trip traumatic.[25]

In a foreign country, in the fresh air (an airplane) at sea, you feel a strange aloofness of everything. A reconsideration of your whole life, a revision of the soul. Suddenly you look at your whole life from aside, as in the minute of death.

How excruciating...

Am I afraid? Of course, I am afraid, I feel terror, but

keep it in check...

I am extremely tense (the language, the responsibilities, the suit, the foreign countries), on the other hand I am outside time and space and free of everything as never before (aloof).[26]

The conference was held in the London Day Training College in Southampton Row (now the Institute of Education, University College London), and Vygotsky was given a seat in the front row, because he was an official Russian delegate. But he felt depressed and alienated, although incredibly proud of being a revolutionary Russian:

Russia is the first country in the world. The Revolution is our supreme cause. In this room only one person knows the secret of the genuine education of the deaf-mutes. And that person is me. Not because I am more educated than the others, but [because] I was sent by Russia and I speak on behalf of the Revolution.[27]

On the last afternoon of the conference Vygotsky gave the final speech:

I salute the conference in the name of the Socialist Soviet Republics of Russia and in the name of the Commissioners of the Russian People for Public Education. I thank the committee for the reception in London, and I trust that the discussions of the conference will have real success.[28]

The Conference delegates were taken to the Royal School for the Deaf in Margate, where the deaf-mute students performed an opera, which Vygotsky watched, "lying on the playing field".

During his London stay he also visited the National Gallery, which he seemed to find disappointing because he thought it lacked many major Western artists. He also visited County Hall,

Parliament, Westminster Abbey, the British Museum and the Lyons' Tea House in Piccadilly. On his way to London and back he visited Gestalt colleagues and other academics in special educational needs in Germany, Holland and France.

Ad for the conference Vygotsky attended in London in 1925

On his return to Russia, he focused on preparing for his viva for his doctoral thesis on *The Psychology of Art* at Moscow State University. In this thesis, Vygotsky wanted to show how art, mainly in the forms of theatre and literature, can be seen in social-cultural terms, affecting emotions, or as a mode for developing thought, the seeds of ideas he was to develop the rest of his life. But, in 1928, he was unable to present his viva for his doctorate owing to a serious attack of tuberculosis, which landed him in hospital for six months. His dissertation was however accepted and he was given a doctorate.

Vygotsky's serious bouts of tuberculosis affected him physically and mentally. He had a nasty attack following his visit to London in 1926. In a letter to his colleague, Sakharov, on 15 February 1926 he wrote:

I have already been here a week—in large rooms for six severely ill patients, (there is) noise, shouting, no table, etc. The beds are ranged next to each other without any space between them, like in barracks. Added to this I feel physically in agony, morally crushed and depressed.[29]

Three weeks later on 5 March 1926, while recovering in a sanatorium, he wrote to Luria:

...around me there was such a situation all the time, that it (CHECK) was shameful and difficult to take a pen in the hand and impossible to think quietly... I feel myself outside of life, more correctly between life and death: I am not yet desperate, but I have already abandoned all hope.[30]

And yet, despite these very challenging conditions he started to write some of his most significant work from his hospital bed.

The *Notebooks* give a fascinating record of his thinking when he started to develop his sociocultural historical ideas. He wrote up several more ideas for his book *The Psychology of Art* and he started to integrate a Marxist analysis into his theory of consciousness, developing his thoughts about the influence of one's experience and social environment on one's consciousness, and the role of talking and of words and concepts on thinking. These can be seen in the collation of his work in *Mind and Society: the Development of Higher Psychological Processes*.[31] He started to develop his analysis of a Marxist psychological theory which he later published in *The Historical Meaning of the Psychological Crisis*.[32] These ideas are explored in the next chapters of this book.

When he left hospital he continued to teach and research in psychology, working at a variety of institutions. He set up a laboratory for the study of "abnormal" children at a Medical Pedagogical Station in Moscow in 1925-6. A year later he became the director of the Defectology Department in the Scientific Research Institute of the Moscow Second State

University (MSU II), a pro-Soviet, Marxist academy.

He started to write prolifically and to edit other books and articles. The main focus of his work was to "problematise", to unpack and analyse the psychological development of "normal" children. He then applied these ideas in his clinical practices with children and adults with a variety of special educational needs and mental health problems. In 1928, his paper on *Institutions for Children Differing from the Norm* was given a key slot in the *Pedagogical Encyclopedia* (1927-1929). He also joined the editorial board of the journal, *Questions of Defectology*, produced by the MSU II Institute's Defectology Section, giving him an outlet for his research for the many papers he was writing at this time. To gain more medical knowledge he completed three years of medical training.

In 1926, Vygotsky became increasingly interested in how people are shaped by their sociocultural environments, quoting Trotsky on "re-shaping of man" where Trotsky discussed the impact of social revolution on consciousness.[33] Perhaps this reflected Vygotsky's own experience of the impact of the revolution on his political transformation. He wrote of how schooling and the social environment can impact on the developing child. Under capitalism, a child is taught to think and develop in a bourgeois manner, but within a revolutionary educational environment it was possible to "perform revolution's music" and hence establish a new society.[34] Vygotsky was creating a Marxist theory based on *cultural historical psychology*, one that showed the impact of social experiences over time on people's thinking or consciousness.

In 1927 he was lecturing at the Krupskaya Academy for Communist Education. In their editorial comments in the *Notebooks*, Zavershneva and Van der Veer suggest that Vygotsky was beginning to develop a "systemic" approach—an understanding of cognition in terms of the inter-dependence of memory, imagination, attention and creativity. He was applying Austrian/German Gestalt theory, which relates shape or image to learning and meaning-making. He was also formulating his theory of "double stimulation": he was interested in how objects could stimulate memory, like tying a knot in your handkerchief, or simply using pictures to reinforce an idea. He started to look at the role of the "sign", the word, or a symbol that indicates a meaning, and how we absorb these signs into our thinking, and how our speech shapes and reflects our thinking. In this way these signs play a crucial role as "instruments" or "tools" in our thinking. The signs are formed through our need to use them within our sociocultural environment, and so are an outcome of our environment. He applied these "instrumental" methods of using objects to stimulate memory and thinking to the hundreds of children, including those with special needs, with whom he and his colleagues were working. So this was an important new teaching and learning or "paedalogical" method, based on a social theory of learning development and meeting needs, breaking away from chalk and talk, and backed up theoretically.[35] He wrote in his notebook:

> All (verbal) thinking of cultural man is a system of external speech mechanisms ingrown in consciousness, the fourth stage of the instrumental acts. Language is a mnemotechnic tool; memorising the verbal (the verbal type of memory).[36]

By the end of the 1920s Vygotsky was well on the way to formulating his Marxist Psychology based on the proposition of understanding children's development in terms of their thinking, their sociocultural environments and the artefacts, particularly language, that were available to them. He applied this approach theoretically and in his clinical work with children with special needs, which in turn informed his theory.

These ideas will be further investigated in later chapters in this book, where we will see how they can be applied to children's learning or to adults' understandings.

Chapter 2
Vygotsky's Later Years & the Rise of Stalinism

Education was liberated by the Revolutionary Government following the October Revolution. They increased the budget for education tenfold and formal teaching methods were jettisoned for a radical pedagogy in which children were given freedom in the classroom. Teachers were seen as guides rather than instructors, exams were abolished and there was a child-centred approach, drawing on children's prior experience and knowledge. While subject boundaries were collapsed, children learned arts, sciences and technology through a thematic research and problem-based approach. Literacy soared across the population. Vygotsky had a role in these exciting new educational practices, training teachers, giving lectures and advising the Commissariat of Education.

But by 1928 things changed radically. Standardised classes were brought into Soviet classrooms. "Chalk and talk" examination-based methods returned. The individualised developmental teaching and learning practices of the Revolution were in direct opposition to Stalinist education policy. Soviet psychological research and practice were similarly affected. Radical researchers and practitioners were purged.

In 1929 Vygotsky wrote in a letter to five of his students: "We live in a period of geological cataclysms in psychology."[37] At the time, he enjoyed an influential position in Soviet psychology.

He was working collaboratively with colleagues, students and patients in the Experimental Defectological Institute (EDI). He was also collaborating with a range of other researchers, including Luria and Leontiev, developing models for cultural historical psychology. But Stalinism dealt a massive blow to this collaboration across the different branches of psychology.

Vygotsky's work was deeply political. He made frequent references to Lenin's ideas in his work, and collaborated with his old Marxist Shaniavsky University lecturer, the philosopher Blonsky, and with Lenin's wife, Krupskaya in the 1930s, in developing models of apprenticeship learning. While many of his writings on language and semiosis, the process of how we make meanings from visual marks or things, have similar themes to the Marxist semiotics of his Russian contemporaries Volosinov and Bakhtin, with whose work he was familiar, there is no evidence that they actually met.

Vygotsky's frequent references to Trotsky's ideas in his notebooks, writings and lectures. were anathema to Stalinism, which led to his replacement as director of the reorganised EDI, by an ex-teacher who was closer to Stalin's line. Nonetheless, he was able to continue his work at the Institute, practising with disturbed children. He was also focussing more on teaching and lecturing about teaching methods that addressed children's development. He taught and researched at the Herzen Pedagogical Institute in Leningrad, collaborating with others in this field, as well as continuing his work at the EDI.

His studies and lectures analysed the child's development in terms of the interaction between mental and physical development, within the child's social and cultural context. He looked at how a child's endocrine or glandular system, their mental system and nervous systems develop as their cultural environment changes. This new arena of study was called *paedology*. His students, who were trainee teachers, in addition to listening to his lectures, were invited into his clinical practice. The notes of his students in these lectures have recently been collated by David Kellogg in *L S Vygotsky's Pedological Works.*

This work was highly respected by his academic colleagues but rejected by the Stalinist regime. Sadly, when the Dean of the Herzen Pedagogical Institute duplicated Vygotsky's lectures for the students he was subsequently arrested as a "Trotskyite" and shot.[38]

Stalinism opposed a cultural-historical approach to psychological practice. So there was an attempt to polarise the study of psychology and defectology from the practice in clinics and schools. Yasnitsky explains that the Stalinist Purge involved simplifying and separating the number of disciplines in psychological and human sciences.[39] So while in the 1920s there were broadly four levels—Marxist philosophy, General Sciences, Applied Sciences and Social Practices—by the end of the 1930s these were converged into two hybrid levels of psychological sciences—Marxist Philosophy and General Science on the one hand, and Social Practice on the other. This meant that the specialist conferences that analysed and attempted to develop individual branches of psychology were no longer permitted. Yasnitsky suggests that this meant there was a split between the theory of psychology, which was placed in the arena of philosophy and general science, and the empirical practice which was in the other category. The result was that psychological practice could not be informed by the theory and research and *vice versa*.

This attempt to split theory from practice also impacted on Vygotsky's work on special needs. Stalinism considered that the use of social and cultural factors as explanations in the development of the child with special needs did not allow for the positive effects of the Soviet educational institution. The result of all this was to integrate children with special needs into mainstream schooling, isolating the work and research of enlightened psychologists.

Pressure from the Stalinist government led to increasing criticism of Vygotsky's psychological and paedological ideas, with a particular attack on cultural historical theory, and several of his colleagues succumbed to Stalinist pressures and left his group to form a new one, which was more closely aligned with Stalinism. Many of his former collaborators, including Luria, abandoned his project and moved to The Centre for Psychological Research and Discussion in Kharkov, Ukraine. It was impossible for Vygotsky to move there but he did give occasional lectures and examined students. But the Kharkov School, toeing the Stalinist line, was opposed to the cultural historical paedological movement. It was not commensurate with a Stalinist psychology which did not approve of a developmental sociocultural model of practice, and certainly not one that had anything to do with Bolshevism, particularly Trotskyism.

Conferences with other researchers and his students were essential to Vygotsky's work. The Psychological Laboratory of the Academy of Communist Educators was closed down in 1932, depriving him and his collaborators of a venue for their laboratory work and research for conferences.

While Vygotsky was transforming the work of a range of international psychologists into his own Marxist theory, and because he was critical of school testing regimes, he was deemed "un-Marxist", and accused of "menshevising" esteemed philosophers and psychologists. But nonetheless, in addition to his headship of the Department of General and Age Paedology and professorship roles in the Second Moscow Medical Institute, he was appointed as Professor and Head of Department of Paedology of Disturbed Childhood at Moscow State Pedagogic Institute, and now held a professorship at the Herzen Pedagogical Institute. He gave some seminal lectures in these academic settings, which his students wrote up, and which have since been published.

In addition to his research and practice in psychology, Vygotsky maintained his interest in literary activities. During his short life, cultural production flourished in revolutionary Russia. He immersed himself in a variety of literary and other cultural events and mixed with the cultural elite. He was friendly with the film director Eisenstein, with whom he planned projects, and with the poets, Mandelstam and Ehrenburg.[40]

As well as being highly intellectual, Vygotsky was a warm, passionate and witty man. He was committed to the emotional well-being of children. He respected individuality and passion in others. At a lecture in Gomel (1921-23) he said:

> People with great passions, people who accomplish great deeds, people who possess strong feelings, even people with great minds and a strong personality, rarely come out of good boys and girls.[41]

Vygotsky with his wife Roza and daughter Asya

It was his warmth and sincerity, in addition to his brilliance that attracted students and other researchers to his project. One student wrote:

> It is hard to determine what exactly attracted us in the lectures of Lev Semyonovich. Apart from their deep and interesting content we were charmed by his genuine sincerity, the continual striving upwards with which he captivated his listeners, (and) the beautiful literary expression of his thought. The sound of his soft baritone itself, flexible and rich in intonation, produced a sort of aesthetic delight. You very much wanted to experience the hypnotising influence of his speech and it was difficult to refrain the involuntary feeling of disappointment when it stopped.[42]

In early 1934, Vygotsky was in the process of attempting to develop a department for clinical psychology at the Moscow-based All-Union Institute for Experimental Medicine, where he worked with Luria and others. But sadly he fell seriously ill again. Vygotsky suffered several tuberculosis haemorrhages in May and June 1934, and died in a sanatorium in Moscow on 11 June. Luria wrote:

> This death was even more tragic given that Lev Semon-ovich died amongst everyone's devotion and love, for the first time in his life being on the verge of bringing all his plans to life and gathering the organised group of researchers he had been dreaming about all his life and who could undertake the realisation of everything that was hidden in the brain of a genius.[43]

By the time of his death Vygotsky had become very unpopular with the Stalinist regime. His admiration for and reference to Trotsky, the psychological and educational fields about which he researched, wrote and taught, were disdained by the regime, which had also become increasingly antisemitic. Van der Veer suggests that had he not died of tuberculosis, Vygotsky, like the dean of his school who had duplicated his lectures, would probably have been sent by the Stalinist regime to die in the Gulag Archipelago.[44]

Chapter 3
The Development of a Marxist Psychology

In 1917 Vygotsky started to apply a Marxist analysis in his work. He also worked, proudly, for the new Revolutionary Government. The editors of the two mainstream English language editions of Vygotsky books, Thought and Language and Mind in Society, cut out many of Vygotsky's references to Marx and Trotsky. Vygotsky's Marxism has only started to be adequately addressed since the year 2000. Therefore, little is generally known about this important aspect that underpinned all of Vygotsky's important ideas.

His political zeal shines through his early work when he was teaching labourers in the evenings and training the teachers of Gomel in the daytime. His lectures were written up in *Educational Psychology*, first published in 1926. He wrote of how schooling and the social environment can impact on the developing child and that the revolution provided exciting opportunities for thinking and learning.

His attempt to develop a Marxist psychology began in earnest in 1925, when psychology was a new science and a range of theories was being developed at an international level.

Vygotsky wanted to take the best from these theories to create a new Marxist psychological theory. He started to look to Marx's method of developing economic theory in *Capital*. In 1927, he wrote in the *Historical Meaning of the Crisis in*

Psychology: "Psychology is in need of its own *Das Kapital*— its own concepts of class, basis, value etc—in which it might express, describe and study its object." He wrote that he wanted to "...find out how science has to be built, to approach the study of mind having learnt the whole of Marx's *method*...".

> In order to create such an enabling theory-method in the generally acceptable scientific manner, it is necessary to discover the essence of the given area of the phenomena, the laws according to which they change, their qualitative and quantitative characteristics, their causes. It is necessary to formulate the categories and concepts that are specifically relevant to them—in other words, to create one's own *Capital*.

> The whole of *Capital* is written according to the following method: Marx analyses a single living "cell" of capitalist society, for example the nature of value. Within this cell he discovers the structure of the entire system and all its economic institutions... Anyone who could discover what a "psychological" cell is—the mechanisms producing even a single response—would thereby find the key to psychology as a whole.[45]

Prior to writing this paper, in 1925, Vygotsky had been looking at how a psychology based on the dominant stimulus-response theory could not account for a theory of "human" behaviour because this did not allow for consciousness. He drew on Marx's famous analogy of the spider and the architect:[46]

> The spider that weaves his web and the bee that builds his cell out of wax do this out of instinct, mechanically, always in the same way, and in doing so they never display any more activity than in any other adaptive reactions. But the situation is different with a weaver or an architect. As Marx said, they first built their works

in their heads; the result of their labours existed before this labour in ideal form.[47]

This differentiation between the way an animal reacts and the way a human plans their actions led him to theorise about the differences between human and animal behaviour and thinking. In his notes for T*he Historical Meaning of the Crisis in Psychology*, he started by saying that animals and humans are different in that humans can use language—they can read, write and talk—whereas the dog merely salivates to a stimulus. So the stimulus-response theories are inadequate in explaining human behaviour. He looking to work out a theory of consciousness and of language, that showed how consciousness has a social origin and that speech has a major function in the development of consciousness. He wanted to develop a dialectical materialist psychology that showed the intersection of speech, consciousness and social interaction. So he looked into Marx's work for the essence of a person as a social formation.

Higher and lower mental functions

The notion of the conscious, thinking man, in control of his actions, with higher mental capabilities, was a popular Marxist view in revolutionary Russia when Vygotsky was developing his analysis. He introduced the categories of *higher and lower mental functions* to account for human consciousness. Higher mental functions refer to the distinctly human mental processes that are *conscious* processes, involving deliberate activity of the mind, where humans can deliberate on their actions and thinking. Essentially, these processes involve the use of signs —language, and visual or auditory meaningful symbols. So a higher mental process may relate to reading or writing or to reasoning, or developing new concepts, all aspects that relate to consciousness.

Lower mental functions are more akin to reflex reactions, "involuntary attention", when we automatically focus on something, or perform a bodily reflex movement. Lower mental functions are the type of reactions we might have in common with animals. This differentiation enabled him to develop a psychological theory applicable to humans and to move away from the reflexological, stimulus-response interpretation of the mind, which assumed that humans act and react like animals.

Because *higher mental processes* (conscious thinking processes) *are mediated through the use of signs*, they are *socially or culturally shaped*. Not only are words, signs and tools shaped by histories and culture and social milieu, our use of these signs involve our thought processes. So our thinking has its origins in the external social world. This sociocultural impact on signs and words—the tools we use for communication—dialectically influences individual thought. When we assimilate, understand and are able to use a concept it becomes part of our thinking kit for further understandings and thought.

Developing a new psychology

The *Notebooks* that he wrote from his sick bed in the Zakharino Hospital in 1926 provide us with a fascinating account of the development of his new psychology theory, which he finally wrote up in 1927 in the *Historical Meaning of the Crisis in Psychology.* These writings, in note-form like the inner speech he was later to theorise about, show how he thought through the rudiments of his theory. Drawing on Marx's analysis in *A Contribution to the Critique of Political Economy,* he was searching for a dialectical materialist model that investigated the interplay between mind and body, biology and consciousness, and between the individual and the society in which a person lives. He found that language is a crucial factor in thinking.

Language and consciousness

He started to look into thinking and speech, a theory that he continued to develop for the rest of his life. The *Notebooks* have many references to Marx. As he began to unscramble his thoughts, he referred to the Marxist notion of *commodity fetishism* in terms of the relationship between a word and the object that it represents. Marx used this concept to show how the human input into production and the social relationships of labour are not accounted for when analysing economic concepts, such as the value of a commodity. Vygotsky used it to show that studying words or language without reference to the social situation, and the speakers and listeners, in which language arises, fetishises words by removing them from their social context. Language becomes an object, with rules disconnected to its users or creators. This is a perspective that should be understood by all teachers, because it is not applied in the current literacy, grammar and spelling strategies, which isolate words from meanings and context.

He wrote in the *Notebooks*

> The word is not a relationship between the sound and the object it denotes. It is a relationship between a speaker and a listener, a relationship between people directed toward an object, it is an interpsychical reaction, which establishes the unity of two organisms in one direction toward the object. Linguistics makes the word into a fetish; the psychologist reveals that behind the visible relationships between things are relationships between people (*cf,* Marx, commodity fetishism). It denotes the unity of the reactions of two persons or two reactions but not of two stimuli.[48]

He proceeded to look to Marx, this time in *The German Ideology*, to think about how language and consciousness interrelate. He still wanted to prove the inadequacy of the stimulus-response models for analysing humans who, unlike animals, have consciousness and language. Referring to Marx and to other psychologists, Vygotsky noted that:

> Consciousness is speech for oneself, it originates in society with language (Marx). The unconscious is what is separated from the word (Freud), consciousness

is verbalised behavior (Watson). A risky idea: bio is unconscious, socio is conscious. Speech is always a dialogue (Shcherba). Consciousness is a dialogue with oneself. Already the fact that the child first listens and understands and then acquires verbal consciousness points out that: (1) Consciousness develops from experience; (2) Speaking with himself = consciously acting, the child takes the position of the other, relates to himself as to another person, imitates another person speaking to him, replaces the other person in relation to himself, learns to be another person in relation to his proper body...[49]

So Vygotsky suggested that we think in language, and that language necessarily involves a speaker and a listener, even if that person is oneself. It comes from the society in which we live, and the social environment in which the speaker is situated. Our experiences influence our consciousness and our thinking. Vygotsky later developed this interactive model of language in *Thought and Language*. (This is covered in a later chapter.)

He then showed the relationship between the thinking conscious mind and the corporeal body:

...generally, mind is the perception of intracorporeal and intranervous experience, it is the organisation of intracorporeal experience. Therefore, fear is to paleness as the sensation of sweetness is to the solution of sugar; fear and sweetness are secondary, reflected, subject-bound, ie intra-organic phenomena. The special properties of mental phenomena can be fully explained from their experiential origin.[50]

This was the start of Vygotsky's holistic Marxist psychology, connecting the mind and body, which underpinned the paedological theory that he developed in the 1930s. It also provided a useful analytical basis for his practical psychological work where he was interested in a person's social history as well as their physiological health and development.

He concluded here that Marx did not actually produce a scientific theory of the mind, relating sensations to experience and consciousness. But Marx could provide a *method*, such as his theory in *Capital,* that accounted for the *appearances* and *essence* of things.

Mediational tools

Essential to Vygotskian theory is the mediational role of language—it mediates our thinking; we think via the use of language. So words act as *tools* for thinking. He used the tool metaphor not only in the physical sense, such as the spade used in the garden that helps us transform the ground, but in the psychological sense. We might write a note or depict images of the world in a variety of symbolic forms, such as maps. These act as mnemonics—to remind ourselves of something. In this way, these signs become tools for our mental activity.

In *Capital*, Marx described man as a tool-making animal who, unlike animals, is able to control nature. In a lecture to the Krupskaya Academy in 1930, Vygotsky showed how, in our tool use, not only are we able to do more things, including using the tool itself more effectively, but that the *psychological tool* can act as a prop, mediating and facilitating our thinking processes. Such tools "are directed toward the mastery of (mental) processes—one's own or someone else's—just as technical devices are directed toward the mastery of processes of nature". Examples of such tools include "language, different forms of numeration and counting, mnemotechnic techniques, algebraic symbolism, works of art, writing, schemes, diagrams, maps, blueprints, all sorts of conventional signs, etc".[51]

Tools enable us to make shortcuts in our actions and thinking. The knot in the handkerchief that we tie as a reminder means that we do not have to go through a series of thought processes to remember something. The representation of the number eight—the sign 8—enables us to immediately make calculations without having to count up eight objects.

The physical tools that we use are made within particular social environments to meet particular needs, so they are formed socially. Similarly, the examples that Vygotsky uses as mental tools are also socially shaped to meet needs. For example, a variety of diagrams have been created to meet specific needs, such as for this book. It has a socially constructed format, intentionally using a Russian Futurist style of image, colour and font, which conveys information in a metaphoric way that this is a book related to that period; so it is understood within this specific social context. Such mental tools mediate our thinking and behaviour by representing meanings.

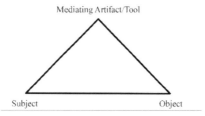

Vygotsky's Mediation Triangle

Vygotsky used a triangle to explain this mediational process in terms of stimulus and response. He suggested that in un-mediated, "natural processes", such as natural memory, we might see A, the stimulus, which reminds us of B, the response. But where we use a psychological tool such as a handkerchief or other form of sign, such as a word or number, which we could call X, instead of the direct association between A and B, the handkerchief or sign mediates the memory of B.

He called this process the *Instrumental Method*. It proved to be very adaptable for his developing psychological theory because it could also be used to show how language can be used as a mental tool to mediate thought.

So by applying this theory to the tools of the mind, we can also say that because all material and ideological tools are shaped by culture and mediate our thoughts, all our thoughts are shaped by the culture in which we live. The words and symbols, as well as the physical implements, have all developed through use in a specific culture, over time. They have a history and a context. Hence, our own thoughts and the words we use are all shaped by this context, history and culture. This theory also explains that the consciousness of each human being needs to be understood within a social and cultural context.

Vygotsky added a historical materialist dimension to this theory by drawing on the work of his Marxist colleague, Blonsky, who focussed on behaviourism, and said that we need to understand behaviour in terms of the history of behaviour and the social context in which it takes place. This allows us to understand the how and why of behaviour. It can be applied to education, unifying the development of the child with his or her education, because it allows us to look at the impact of education on a child, because we can look at the child's history and social context and how his or her learning changes in the process of education.

In developing this theory Vygotsky cites Marx in terms of how tools facilitate mental development. In the process of development man "changes his own nature... develops the forces slumbering in it and subordinates the play of forces to his own power".[52] It also demonstrates how "...the use of signs leads humans to specific structures of behaviour that breaks away from biological development and creates new forms of a culturally-based psychological process".[53]

Conclusion

It is generally thought that Vygotsky was successful in developing a new and important Marxist-based psychology. Using a sociohistorical dialectical method he was able to show how our consciousness is shaped by mental and social experiences over time. Tools, in the form of a variety of signs, play an essential role in this process by facilitating our thinking. His later work rested on and developed this perspective.

Chapter 4
The Acquisition of Language & Concept Development

Marx and Engels wrote in *The German Ideology*:

> Language is as old as consciousness, language is practical consciousness that exists also for other men, and for that reason alone it really exists for me personally as well; language, like consciousness, only arises from the need, the necessity, of intercourse with other men.[54]

Marx and Engels showed how as human beings we develop the use of language from the need to communicate with others in the course of our daily living, in the process of collecting or obtaining food, of working, etc.

Vygotsky went much further. He demonstrated how language is a tool for our thinking; it mediates our thinking. It is deeply social, not only because it is used for social intercourse, but because it is formed within a social context. This proposition is at the heart of his work.

Language and thinking

In 1926, Vygotsky started to look into the relationship between thinking and speech, an area of theory that he continued to develop for the rest of his life. As we have seen, his notebooks on this theme have several references to Marx.

He had studied linguistics at university and it played a major role in his PhD thesis. He later said that the subject of linguistics *fetishises* words because it does not take on board the social context. Psychology should look at the *social relationships* involved in language use—the speaker, the listener, the context in which the communication takes place.

As a Marxist psychologist, Vygotsky was interested in the *genesis*, meaning the origins and the history of the development of the child's thinking, within the context of her social and interactive experiences. This involved a long and intensive study of how language impacts on thinking. The child's social and cultural environment has a crucial role to play in her cognitive development.

A child generally does not use language until the age of two or three. Until that age they use some form of utterance, like a cry or another sound, to communicate a need or a response, or a greeting. Once the child starts to string words together they are able to use words as a tool for thinking. Vygotsky wrote in *Thought and Language*:[55]

> The acquisition of language can provide a paradigm for the entire problem of the relation between learning and development. Language arises initially as a means of communication between the child and the people in his environment. Only subsequently, upon conversion to internal speech, does it come to organise the child's thought, that is, become an internal mental function.[56]

This statement sums up the significant role that language plays in our thinking. Once we are able to think in language, using *inner speech*, it becomes a tool for thinking. It mediates our thinking because it provides a means for thinking.

Vygotsky's ideas about concepts show how language enhances thinking and development. The notion of a concept refers to an abstract idea that usually has a word or phrase to name it. As a child or adult learns a new concept it is *internalised* into her thinking process. It can then be used to think through new ideas. For example, once you understand what "evolution" is you use the concept to develop an understanding of a related concept such as "natural selection". Once you have an understanding of racism, you can make some sense of *apartheid*. But the way we understand the meaning of a concept deepens as we mature and become familiar with the term.

The vital role of concepts in the learning process, and the development of understanding of concepts, makes this aspect of Vygotsky's work particularly important for educators. It shows the importance of language in cognitive development. It also introduces us to the range of concepts, and their relevance to teaching and learning.

Concept development

Vygotsky distinguished between different types of concepts. He showed the significance of the concepts we learn in our daily life and those used in schooling experiences and he showed how concepts are developed. He described in detail the stages that the child goes through from a very vague or *syncretic* notion of the meaning of a concept when they begin to talk, to a full and deeper understanding during adolescence and in adult life.

In his analysis of the development of concepts, which he established from observations of children, Vygotsky again drew on the dialectical and historical relationship between language and thinking. He showed how a child's understanding of concepts is *gradual*. A child or adult does not immediately have a full comprehension of a new concept, but starts with a "*protoconcept*", an unformed concept or rough idea of the meaning, which as the child matures they are able to transform into a true concept, which can operate in her thinking. Vygotsky believed that while the very young child begins to use those processes that develop her concept formation, the psychological operations involved in deeper understanding really only begin to function as real intellectual processes in the teenage years.

It is interesting to watch young children develop an understanding of the concept of time, using the concept of *later*, or *day* and *night*. Children of three or four years of age can use these concepts appropriately, in a *protoconceptual* form, but would be unlikely to use the more complex notion of time.

Vygotsky pointed out that the language used by young children is often taught or told to them by an adult. Words come from the society in which we live, and each individual needs to learn the meaning of those words. The progression of understanding of concepts is slow and developmental. As adults we know this. When we meet a new concept, we do not immediately understand what the term means. We need someone to give us concrete examples of the concept. We then start to test the term out, to apply it in a variety of contexts to see if we have the right meaning. Eventually we can use it confidently and appropriately in other contexts. We have grasped the true concept!

Vygotsky based his research on concept development on experiments with over 300 "subjects"—adults, teenagers, children and patients with mental health challenges. His observations helped him to develop his theory of how children form concepts.

Blocks Experiment[57]

He used 22 blocks of different colours, shapes, height and sizes in his observations of how the subjects group objects with common categories.[58] They are coloured red, blue, green, yellow and white. But there are four categories, denoted by nonsense words—*lag*—tall and fat blocks, *bik*—small and fat blocks, *mur*—tall and thin blocks, and *cev*—small and thin—on the reverse of each block. The children were not told that there were four words representing the complex concepts, nor did they know that these words actually refer to a combination of the height and the size of the object.

The subjects were asked to organise the blocks into groups. As they did so, they used *egocentric speech*, expressing their thoughts aloud about which block should go with others. Egocentric speech is the private but verbalised speech, particularly of young children. You can hear this when they play with toys in the bath or their cot. Some of us also use it as adults when trying to resolve a problem.

Vygotsky's desk with some of the blocks he used in his observations

Vygotsky found that when presented with these blocks, the young child tended to group them in random heaps, with no clear notion as to the category or concept that the blocks in each heap shared. An adult might place a group of blocks together and assign the word *yellow* or *green* etc to them, but the child's understanding of the meaning of *yellow* is vague, what Vygotsky called *syncretic*. The young child placing objects in the yellow pile tends to do so through a chance impression, dependent on which objects are closest to her. Objects are linked or classified in a seemingly arbitrary way. But this arbitrariness acts as a hypothetical experiment for the child as she makes meanings from her world. So if told they have made a mistake in their classification, another block may be placed in the pile through a random process.

The child at this age uses the same category for a multitude of objects. For example, the child may have a dog in the home called Fido and may well call all dogs Fido, or all four-legged animals Fido. They have not learnt that this particular dog is called Fido, is a *dog*, and that *dog* refers to a particular genus of animal. Their perception at this age is immature and *syncretic* and their thinking is at the trial and error stage. As they progress through this stage, categorisation tends to be based on the situation they are in. The use of concepts is applied to visible objects, whereas adults can conceptualise without the concrete presence of the concept.

At the second stage of concept development, the child is able to see a bond between the concept and the object. They group objects that are connected in some conceptual way— colour or shape or size, etc. Therefore the child is able to *think in complexes*. Instead of basing her judgements on her individual impression, the child is moving away from egocentrism and able to think objectively. Her thinking is still unlike adult thinking which is, on the whole, conceptual rather than in complexes. Vygotsky compared this stage to the way we use surnames, or family names. If Petrov is the family name then all members of that family will be thought of as having that name: each person will be thought of as being called Petrov. The child, *thinking in complexes*, assigns all objects that are similar to a family name in the same way. They are still using concrete, factual bonds, or relations, to group objects under the same concept, rather than the logical reasoning that adults are able to do.

As the child matures through this stage they begin to be able to group different objects which have a characteristic in common, and hence the family name applies to a variety of different objects, sharing a similar feature. They understand that this is a dog called Fido, and their friend's dog is called Bruno. At the end of the thinking in complexes stage the child is able to group objects in terms of their *difference*. Therefore a blue, a red and a green block may be grouped together because they differ in colour. However they are all blocks. The child is able to understand that spoons, forks and knives are all eating utensils, although different. In their verbal thinking they can show that they are a functional group, complementing each other. Vygotsky called this the *collection complex*. Throughout this thinking in complexes stage the child continues to relate different objects based on concrete experiences.

Before they reach the true conceptual stage, the child, while appearing to use conceptual thought, is in fact still using a process similar to that of thinking in complexes. Vygotsky's experiments showed that the child was still using visual clues of similarity to group objects. He called this type of complex a *pseudoconcept*, which is the most usual form of complex thinking of the pre-school child.

Vygotsky's Blocks

Vygotsky found that when asked to group yellow triangles, the child grouped every object that was triangular, including polygons that might have looked like a triangle with the top cut off. He concluded that the child had not grasped the mental, abstract concept, but still relied on concrete, visual perception. Thus the *word meaning* is not the same as the *mental concept*, because the child applies the word but does not use the same mental operations as an adult would. Eventually through interactions with adults, the child's understandings mature into the formation of real, mental concepts. The development of the ability to think in complexes helps the child to organise her thinking, moving from a concept based on a vague collection of impressions into an organisation in discrete groups, which later forms the basis for generalisations in a more abstract sense.

The adolescent, given an appropriate environment that reinforces social, linguistic and mental development is then able to use concepts in their thought, and to be able to generalise.

Thus concepts, words and phrases which express an idea, are learnt through an evolving process. "Word meanings evolve" and "a concept embodied in a word represents an act of generalisation".[59] In other words, the word itself is not concrete but a *generalisation*, and is initially related to concrete situations. Gradually the generalisation becomes increasingly sophisticated which leads to the formation of true concepts.

The blocks experiment provides a fascinating display of how thinking takes place. In another experiment with them, two people are given the blocks to sort, having been shown one of the nonsense categories written underneath them. They are asked to express their thought in words as to which groups they think the blocks belong to. Gradually they are shown the other categories under the blocks. Observation of the communicative exchanges, and spoken thinking process and the consequent actions that take place exposes how those people think, how they negotiate, how they listen, how they might take on, or not, the suggestions of their partner. In short, you can observe Vygotsky's analysis of inter/intractive processes in action. In other words, it shows the impact of talking between people—*inter*—on the individual internal thinking process—*intra*. (This can also occur when verbalising thoughts that become internal unverbalised thought.) This experiment provides a challenge to people of all ages, and is an excellent demonstration of concept formation.

Two types of concepts

Like other sociocognitive educationalists (such as Bernstein, Cummins and Mercer), Vygotsky distinguished between the concepts that we learn in our daily experience—*spontaneous* or *everyday concepts* — and those that we are taught in the schooling or academic context—*scientific* or *academic concepts*. This distinction is important because he showed how we learn these two types of concepts differently. Since academic success is dependent on understanding academic concepts, an understanding of how they are learned can inform how we teach. This theory also helps us to understand why and how sociocultural background impacts on learning.

We have a closer relationship to everyday concepts because we have direct, personal experience with them. On the other hand, *scientific concepts* are outside our daily experience; in order to know them we have to be taught them directly, by a teacher or a more knowledgeable peer, or through reading.

Personal experience and previous knowledge help to give children deeper understanding of new concepts. In learning a new scientific concept the teacher tends to introduce the concept, defines it and gives examples of its use. In *Thought and Language* Vygotsky gives the example of asking a student about *revolution*.

> ...when asked about revolution, a third-grader, who already learned at school about the Russian revolutions of 1905 and 1917, answers, 'Revolution is a war of the exploited against the exploiters' or 'This is a civil war, citizens of one country fight each other'. One finds a sign of the development of consciousness and the class criterion in these answers. But the conscious understanding of subject differs here essentially, in terms of penetration and comprehension, from the understanding of adults.[60]

It appears as if the student in this example is repeating a definition but the additional explanation shows a deeper understanding, which is perhaps not equivalent to some more knowledgeable adults, who might give a more detailed answer, or explain the process in abstract terms, or give more examples with clarifications. As people mature they can add a depth of knowledge to their interpretation of an academic concept to create an increasingly sophisticated understanding.

He compared this to a child defining the concept of "brother" who was "completely captured by the logic of actual situations and cannot approach this concept as an abstract one".[61] At this syncretic level of understanding, the student is unable to generalise the concept.

Vygotsky describes the learning process of academic concepts as operating "downwards", because the child is introduced to the concept externally, as a word, not necessarily experientially, and gradually connects it to concrete, known examples. Concepts are "complex thought acts" so they cannot be properly taught simply through drilling. Students need to engage with these concepts, attempt to see how they fit with their current knowledge and experience. Further, they should only be introduced when the child is mentally ready to learn them. On the other hand, spontaneous, or everyday, concepts are learned through social experiences and interactions: they are learnt "upwards". Thus he observed:

> The development of the child's spontaneous concepts proceeds upwards, and the development of his scientific concepts downwards. This is a consequence of the different ways in which the two kinds of concepts emerge. The inception of a spontaneous concept can usually be traced to a face-to-face meeting with a concrete situation, while a scientific concept involves from the first a "mediated" attitude towards its object.[62]

So the spontaneous concept is learned through everyday actions, while the academic concept is explicitly taught.

Vygotsky uses this relationship as the basis for his commitment to the importance of "*systematic learning*" in the "development of schoolchildren".[63] His analysis of concept development means that for successful teaching, teachers should be aware of the concepts that are embedded in their teaching and aware of whether or not pupils are familiar with, know, or understand them. They need to use sensitive direct teaching methods in order for their pupils or students to make sense of new concepts, vital to intellectual development. His theory relating to scientific concepts has often been ignored by progressive teachers who have erroneously believed that activity-based learning, learning through experience, or a "pick-up" pedagogy, facilitates learning. It is spontaneous everyday concepts that are learnt through experience.

Vygotsky's theory of scientific concepts allowed him to distinguish between the assimilation of knowledge and what he called the "internal development of a scientific concept", the child's understanding of the concept. He critiqued current theorists of his time for failing to understand the way in which concept-learning has a "history", that there is a maturation in the development of understanding. A child's understanding of concepts only occurs when the child is at the appropriate stage of development. At first the concept is always a generalisation, and at an early age this is understood at a very basic level. As the child matures, they have more concepts and other understandings that they can use to develop their intellect at an increasingly higher level. Once academic concepts have been understood they act as a resource to learn new ones. Vygotsky says that they start to be more like everyday concepts.

We can extend Vygotsky's ideas about concept learning to understanding underachievement in children who come from home environments which are less language-rich than ones that use more elaborate language on a daily basis. A child from a more language-rich environment will have learnt more academic concepts than one who comes from a less articulate environment. They will therefore have a more extensive conceptual understanding upon which they can understand new concepts.

Wayne Au has written an interesting piece that explains Vygotsky's notions of "academic" and "everyday" concepts, how they relate to consciousness and how they are learnt by relating them to Lenin teaching the proletariat about revolution.[64] In *What is to be Done* Lenin wrote of the education of the proletariat, particularly in terms of class consciousness.[65] This concept would have been an academic concept to them prior to their experience of a revolution. Au concluded that Vygotsky's conception of conscious awareness and scientific concepts correlates with Lenin's conception of consciousness. Au likens Vygotsky's "everyday" concepts with Lenin's "spontaneous" working-class consciousness, and Vygotsky's academic concepts with Lenin's "conscious" working-class consciousness. Hence, when Lenin was educating the proletariat about revolution, this to them was a complex notion, beyond their own everyday knowledge and experience. It had to be explicitly taught, by relating to their previous knowledge and experience and using explanation processes that relate to Vygotsky's notion of the *zone of proximal development*.[66] Au thus provides an interesting and useful comparison which elaborates and elucidates the theories of both men. Vygotsky, who frequently used Lenin's ideas but who never met him, would probably have appreciated this.

Conclusion

Vygotsky's proposal that the child's thinking processes originate in the social world broke away from the more cognitivist, isolationist view held by Swiss psychologist Jean Piaget and his followers. Vygotsky's analysis showed how the child's social environment is essential to their consciousness and thinking, from the moment they can use language as a toddler. He draws our attention to the role of concepts, underpinning the whole learning process, because they hold the meaning of words.

This analysis of the development of language and thinking, while seemingly complex at first, is essential if we are to have an understanding of how children develop, how rationality develops, and how the social environment impacts on the cognitive development of the child. If the child develops in a social world in which they experience and are able to make sense of more elaborate concepts, this necessarily means that their thinking and use of language will be more elaborate than the child raised in a less stimulating environment.

The differentiation between spontaneous or everyday concepts and the academic concepts taught in the educational context has significant repercussions for anybody concerned with teaching and learning. Furthermore it provides a basis for explaining why so many pupils struggle in school. Where children live in environments which use less elaborate or academic-related concepts, they will have to learn more academic concepts than those who come from backgrounds that use language and thinking processes that are closer to the dominant discourses used in schooling.

The onus on educators to be aware of the processes of the development of concepts cannot be overstated. Most new learning involves the internalisation of new concepts. There are important pedagogical implications for teachers.

The vitally important mediational and developmental role that language plays in the evolution of thought underpinned all Vygotsky's work, as we shall see in the following chapters.

Chapter 5
Learning, Testing & Teaching

Vygotsky's view of learning is essentially a social one based on the interaction between the learner and other people in their social and material environment. This environment shapes our thinking, mainly through the medium of language. It is also necessarily a cognitive one, in which learning is understood to take place through a process of mediation, that is, through language. In developing this theory of learning, as with the rest of his psychological research, Vygotsky drew on a range of other thinkers.

Collaborative thinking
We have seen in previous chapters how language and the concepts through which we think are socially formed. So our thinking is rooted within a sociocultural context and is developed through social interaction using signs. Interaction underpins much of Vygotsky's analysis of how we learn and develop.

He called communication with another person an *interpsychological* process, the *inter* part of the word referring to communication and thought between people. He described the individual thinking process as *intrapsychological*, where the *intra* refers to inside or inner thinking processes. He therefore proposed, in *Mind in Society* and in *Thought and Language*, that the process of communication with other people is vital to our individual thought processes.

When we have a discussion with someone, we express our inner thinking, our intrapersonal thoughts, which have formed through social intercourse or experience. In the discussion the ideas that are shared between people become interpersonal. The ideas then may impact on the participants' thinking, changing or developing their thinking, becoming intrapersonal. In Vygotsky's words:

> *An interpersonal process is transformed into an intrapersonal one.* Every function in the child's cultural development appears twice: first on the social level, and later, on the individual level; first, *between* people (*interpsychological*), and then *inside* the child (*intrapsychological*). This applies to voluntary attention, to logical memory and to the formation of concepts. All the higher functions originate as actual relations between human individuals.[67]

So, through social interactions a child or adult *internalises* the other's thoughts into their own thought processes and uses them as mental tools for further thinking.

Through such an interactive use of the notion of *internalisation* it is possible to see the influence of Freudianism in Vygotsky's thinking. But he went much further because of his account of mediation, differentiation between tool and sign, and his distinction between higher and lower mental processes. This linkage, or dialectical relationship, between language, thinking, consciousness and the social environment of the child or adult was a deeply significant contribution to theories of child development.

Thinking through egocentric speech

Intra-active communication theory shows how our thinking develops through interaction. Talking plays an important role in the development of thinking.

Vygotsky suggested that there are various levels of

thought-related speech. Young children think aloud, using words, in what he termed *egocentric speech*. As they mature they are able to internalise their thoughts verbally, which he called *verbal thought*. And eventually they are able to think as adults do, without language, using *inner speech.*

In the blocks experiment in the last chapter we saw how children began to work out the complex concepts with which the blocks were labelled through speech, where they were externalising their thought processes, thinking aloud, using "egocentric speech", a term introduced by Vygotsky's contemporary Jean Piaget.

As the child matures their use of language plays an increasingly significant role in their thinking process. Between the ages of two and seven, they are able to use words to communicate to others. They also use language to express their thinking aloud, to themselves, thereby using what Vygotsky called "external operations" to solve "internal operations".[68] This is often done while playing, where children seem to whisper or talk to themselves while sorting their toys in specific orders, or planning how to arrange them. In such instances they use language to solve problems, to work things out, intra-actively, inside their heads. Vygotsky gives the example of the child using their fingers to count, or other objects as aids, mnemonics, to memorise things.

Vygotsky's theory of egocentric speech shows us how as individuals we think our thoughts aloud, and in the process language is used to mediate thinking. He applied this theory particularly to children's thinking development. If you listen to children talking to themselves as they play with toys, the words they use may not make sense to another person, although it is part of their playing and thinking process. This is because:

> Egocentric speech… is speech on its way inwards, inti-
> mately tied up with the ordering of the child's behav-
> iour, already partly incomprehensible to others, yet
> still overt in form.[69]

Egocentric speech plays a highly significant role in the development of the child because of its role in scaffolding the child's thinking in resolving complicated tasks:

> The more complex the action demanded by the situation and the less direct its solution, the greater the importance played by speech in the operation as a whole. Sometimes speech becomes of such vital importance that without it the child proves to be positively unable to accomplish the given task.[70]

Adults may also use a form of audible egocentric speech to resolve problems. This might occur, audibly, while driving, for instance. So egocentric speech operates as a prop for thinking. The use of speaking aloud helps the speaker to develop and remember their thinking. It also facilitates the thinking processes as it is internalised.

Vygotsky's analysis of egocentric speech differed from that developed by Piaget, who suggested that children grow out of this phase. Piaget described it as a form of every child's autism, where they live in a rather unsocialised world. Vygotsky, on the other hand, suggested that this is not autistic behaviour but merely individualised thinking. Further, this does not stop at seven as Piaget thought but continues, often maturing into verbal thought or unarticulated *inner speech.*

This inner speech occurs at the fourth stage in language and thought development at what Vygotsky called the in-growth stage. At this time the child begins to use their logical memory, thinking without speaking words aloud and using external signs—symbols, tools and language—as aids to work out meanings and ideas. The internalised language operates as "tools for thinking", creating an inner language.

Inner speech and thought are not the same. Vygotsky argued that thoughts are not expressed in words, since what we say does not necessarily express the totality of what we think:

> Every sentence that we say in real life has some kind
> of subtext, a thought behind it... (Further) just as one
> sentence may express different thoughts, one thought
> may be expressed in different sentences.[71]

It may take several sentences to express one thought, despite it being a brief notion in the speaker's mind because it is present as a multi-layered form. Vera John-Steiner suggests that the notes or jottings that we make to give a lecture might be similar to inner speech since they are in a condensed form. Such a "use of telegraphic styles captures the speed with which clusters of thought emerge".[72]

To show the relationship between speech and thought, Vygotsky used the analogy of two overlapping circles, one representing speech, the other thought. The speech part relates to non-intellectual speech, which does not reflect thinking, for example an exclamation, or everyday statement or question. The area where the circles overlap is represented by what Vygotsky termed *verbal thought,* the expression of thoughts in words, where there is an inter-relationship between thinking and speaking, when speaking facilitates thinking or vice versa. The inner-speech part is the non-verbal thinking, when we think in chunks of ideas, to which words are not attached, but which originated in words.

The development of verbal thought and inner speech are dependent on the child's social and cultural environment, who they communicate with and who they share daily living experiences with, and the purposes for which language and thought are used. The more scientific concepts the child has mastered the more resources they have for thinking. Further, as we have previously seen, the language that we use is shaped by the sociocultural environment, as well as the history of that environment and the experiences we have of it. The more varied the language and cultural environment surrounding the child, the more opportunities they have to develop their thinking, because thinking, language, verbal thought and inner speech have sociohistorical roots. Drawing on Engels' dialectical theory, Vygotsky claimed that:

> Verbal thought is not an innate, natural form of behaviour, but is determined by a historical-cultural process and has specific properties and laws that cannot be found in the natural forms of thought and speech. Once we acknowledge the historical character of verbal thought, we must consider it subject to the premises of historical materialism, which are valid for any historical phenomenon in human society. It is only to be expected that on this level the development of behaviour will be governed essentially by the general laws of the historical development of human society.[73]

The correlation between the development of thought and language and the sociocultural environment has important implications in terms of learning development, educational achievements and motivation. It means that a teacher has to be sensitive to what the child knows and, more importantly for Vygotsky, what the child is capable of knowing. It also means that it is important for teachers and other adults in the child's environment to provide a linguistically rich environment and a variety of engaging experiences.

The Zone of Proximal Development

Vygotsky was committed to the development of children to their full potential. His theory of the Zone of Proximal Development (ZPD) enables us to address teaching and learning in terms of a child's or person's learning *potential*. Essentially it refers to the zone or area of learning of which a child is capable with the assistance of a teacher or "more capable peer". It is therefore a deeply social and collaborative way of understanding children's capabilities and how appropriate adult or peer intervention assists that learning. He showed how this theory was far more constructive and optimistic than testing actual development, which he called "yesterday's development".

The ZPD is based on developing the child for "tomorrow" in the metaphoric sense, focussing on the child's future development. This is a social, historical and cultural theory, imbued with the notion of intra-active learning, and part of his sociocultural, sociohistorical dialectical materialist psychology, not just a one-off teaching technique, as many populist educationalists would have us believe. He wrote:

> The zone of proximal development defines those functions that have not yet matured but are in the process of maturation, functions that will mature tomorrow but are currently in an embryonic state. These functions could be termed the "buds" or "flowers" of development rather than the "fruits" of development.[74]

The use of the metaphors of *buds* developing into *flowers* powerfully and rather beautifully indicates the positive blossoming of a child's development over time.

In order to understand the role of the teacher or more competent peer helping a pupil to learn into their ZPD Jerome Bruner introduced the notion of *scaffolding*, another metaphor. He suggested that the role played by the more knowledgeable collaborating peer or adult is akin to lending one's thinking.

> If the child is enabled to advance by being under the tutelage of an adult or a more competent peer, then the tutor or the aiding peer serves the learner as a vicarious form of consciousness until such time as the learner is able to master his own action through his own consciousness and control. When the child achieves that conscious control over a new function or conceptual system, it is then that he is able to use it as a tool. Up to that point, the tutor in effect performs the critical function of "scaffolding" the learning task to make it possible for the child, in Vygotsky's words,

to internalise external knowledge and convert it into a tool for conscious control.[75]

Vygotsky believed that teachers should always perceive learners in terms of their potential. It is unhelpful to think of the actual developmental level of the learner as this cannot guide a teacher as to what the child is *capable* of doing, given appropriate help. The ZPD therefore describes the child's learning potential, developed through effective adult or peer interaction. Vygotsky wrote of this concept in *Thought and Language* and in *Mind in Society*, and in other publications. He described the ZPD as "...the distance between the actual developmental level as determined by individual problem solving and the level of potential development as determined through problem solving under adult guidance or in collaboration with more capable peers".[76]

Each child has their own potential zone in which they should be taught. This idea is dependent on recognising that the child's potential exists through capabilities that are in the process of development. Effective teaching is seen as providing supportive strategies for helping students to understand. Learning is seen as a social, interactive process, in which more able peers can act as "scaffolders", or supporters, to help less able peers. This scaffolding collaboration between pupils or between the pupil and the teacher can have a significant impact on learning. "What the child can do in co-operation today he can do alone tomorrow."[77] If we reflect on Vygotsky's own development as a child, he clearly enjoyed helping his less competent friends in their learning at school.

Mercer elaborates on this idea by describing the space in which the teacher effectively teaches the child as the "intermental development zone".[78] This zone has its limits, which are shown when the teacher has taught something in a way that is incomprehensible to the child—beyond the child's ZPD—so the child is unable to learn. Likewise, if the teaching is at the child's actual developmental level, then learning will not have taken place. The notion therefore encourages teachers to stretch children, through effectively scaffolding, using an understanding of their potential capabilities.

The ZPD also provides us with a useful tool for understanding how effective mixed ability groupings can provide opportunities to help less able children. Through explaining to their peers, "higher fliers" can deepen and develop their own learning, since the simplification of ideas is a complex thinking and learning process in itself.

This interaction from more to less able peer provides an exchange of language and thought processes which then are used as mental tools by the less able peer for further learning: from the *intermental* zone, between two people, they become *intramental* within the consciousness of the learner. As Vygotsky wrote: "Learning awakens a variety of internal developmental processes that are able to operate only when the child is interacting with people in his environment and in co-operation with his peers."[79]

Group and pair work should not therefore be seen merely as a means of developing "good speaking and listening skills" but as essential strategies in the whole learning process, across the curriculum, through the inter/intra-active process and the impact on the ZPD.

The ZPD also explains how learning takes place in settings outside the school classroom. It shows the importance of talk in the development of understanding at all levels—from the higher education classroom to the nursery setting. If the interaction operates within the child's potential zone, it is likely it will impact on their thinking development.

This notion of collaborative, inter/intra-active learning that underpins the optimistic ZPD informs much of Vygotsky's pedagogy. For him, successful education worked through an effective correlation between the teacher, the learner and the child's social environment. In one of his earliest publications, he wrote:

Education may be defined as a systematic, purposeful, intentional, and conscious effort at intervening in and influencing all those processes that are part of the individual's natural growth.[80]

When teaching a practical skill it is the skill that is the aim of the lesson. It is completely different where an academic subject is concerned, because there is no ceiling to the learning, so it can involve a mentally developmental approach:

We have seen that instruction and development do not coincide. They are two different processes with very complex interrelationships. Instruction is only useful when it moves ahead of development. When it does, it impels or awakens a whole series of functions that are in a state of maturation lying in the zone of proximal development. This is what distinguishes the instruction of the child from the training of animals. This is also what distinguishes instruction of the child which is directed towards his full development from instruction in specialised technical skills such as typing or riding a bicycle. The formal aspect of each subject is that in which the influences of instruction on development are realised. Instruction would be completely unnecessary if it merely utilized what had already matured in the developmental process, if it were not itself a source of development.[81]

Motivational teaching is optimistic teaching, teaching in the child's zone of potential, and teaching for the ongoing development of the student.

The Zone of Proximal Development and testing

Children's development is not the guiding force behind the current testing regime in the UK. Vygotsky exposes the futility of the exam/testing processes as a gauge of pupils potential through this theory. He suggested that:

> Formerly it was believed that by using tests, we determine the mental development level with which education should reckon and whose limits it should not exceed. This procedure oriented learning toward yesterday's development, toward developmental stages already learned.[82]

Summative testing—end of unit tests, or more formal examinations, which supposedly test what a child has learnt —do not in themselves promote learning. We know that such tests are used to label schools, pupils and teachers in a grading game, that commodifies learners. Vygotsky proposed that it is far better to measure pupils' potential by analysing their achievement in a "test" where there is collaboration and hence scaffolding by the teacher. It should be seen as a "joint activity".

He did not propose exactly how the testing was to be done. However, in the Blocks Experiment, the assessor or observer showed the child the name of a random block when they asked the child to group them together. As the child progressed in this task (which many adults can find quite challenging) the assessor scaffolded the process by occasionally showing more of the names on the reverse of the blocks. Thus the observation of the child's capabilities was within a collaborative, scaffolded, interactive context.

Vygotsky was not opposed to all types of symptomatic testing, which he used in some of his assessments. The point he was making was that learning and teaching should be seen as a positive, collaborative activity and that teachers should consider the child in terms of their potential.

Vygotsky distinguished between *symptomatic* and *diagnostic* assessment.

> A symptomatic assessment focuses on behaviours and characteristics... that are typical of children at

a particular psychological type or developmental stage. In contrast, a diagnostic assessment relies on an explicit theory of psychological development in an attempt to penetrate the internal causal dynamic and genetic connections that define the process of mental development.[83]

The use of diagnostic assessment—a type of formative assessment that is included as a part of the teaching process —has been taken up by a variety of educational psychologists and theorists, particularly by followers of Vygotsky working in Russia. Tests have included tasks with teacher prompts, compared to tasks without prompting.[84] In addition, this creates a less stressful environment for assessing learning than the isolated experience of the examination hall.

Collaboration is deeply embedded in the ZPD concept. Vygotsky wrote and talked about how people progress when working collaboratively with more capable peers or adults. This collaborative practice to develop people's ZPD has been taken up by a variety of psychosocial professions.

We need *time* to effectively assess people's and children's potential and in a context that is supportive. In a presentation at a Social Work Action Network conference in 2011, Simon Wey described his approach to the assessment of people with dementia.[85] He was concerned that his service users seemed to be under-performing when they were assessed in an unfamiliar hospital setting. When he changed to a scaffolded ZPD method, assessing his patients in an environment with which they were familiar, such as their own homes, he found that their memory and other abilities functioned more effectively. One patient was able to remember, with the use of memory aid tools within her home environment, where her walking stick was. She was more mobile at home than in the ward, where there were no memory aids. The constructive presence of the assessor was also able to jog her memory, so that she functioned more successfully.

This sort of technique is particularly challenging for social and support workers under the current pressures of tick-box assessments, demands for faster outputs and with inadequate staff numbers. The same may be said within teaching. It is quicker and cheaper to mass test, than to assess scaffolded learning.

Conclusion

The interactive/intra-active collaborative nature of teaching and learning that underpins a Vygotskian approach provides teachers and people who work with other groups with a valuable framework for understanding how people learn and the importance of collaborative learning. The ZPD theory sees the learner in terms of their potential, but also provides an invaluable teaching strategy. It also exposes the testing environment in which we have to work as a sham, a useless exercise that is more aimed at making judgments about funding or for Ofsted criteria than for promoting learning. Bruner wrote of Vygotsky's contribution to our understanding of how children learn:

> A quiet revolution has taken place in developmental psychology in the last decade. It is not only that we have begun to think again of the child as a social being— one who plays and talks with others, learns through interactions with parents and teachers—but because we have come to appreciate once more that through such social life, the child acquires a framework for interpreting experience, and learning how to negotiate meaning in a manner congruent with the requirements of the culture. "Making sense" is a social process; it is an activity that is always situated within a cultural and historical context.

> Before that, we had fallen into the habit of thinking of the child as an "active scientist", constructing hypotheses about the world, reflecting upon experience,

interacting with the physical environment and formulating increasingly complex structures of thought. But this active, constructing child had been conceived as a rather isolated individual, working alone at her problem solving. Increasingly, we see now that, given an appropriate, shared social context, the child seems more competent as an intelligent social operator than she is as a "lone scientist" coping with the world of the unknown.[86]

Chapter 6
Creativity, Imagination, Play & Writing

Imagination

Vygotsky was committed to the best possible development of Russian society and the best possible development of each child. He wanted to establish a revolutionary paedology that met the developmental needs of every Russian child and for a technologically advanced and creative Russian state.

He believed that it is imagination that drives all progress in society. He wrote:

> ...imagination, as the basis of all creative activity, is an important component of absolutely all aspects of cultural life, enabling artistic, scientific, and technical creation alike. In this sense, absolutely everything around us that was created by the hand of man, the entire world of human culture, as distinct from the world of nature, all this is the product of human imagination and of creation based on this imagination.[87]

His key ideas on imagination and play are to be found in a lengthy article he wrote in 1931 and in the write-up of a lecture he gave to the Leningrad Pedagogical Institute in 1933.[88] The article, *Imagination and Creativity in Childhood*, was an extensive study, with reference to a variety of other researchers, analysing the different creative activities in which children use their imagination.[89] He looked at children's play, story writing, drawing, role-play and drama.

For all imaginative endeavours, children and adults draw on the elements of their material experiences in order to create new imaginative ones, to extend and develop what is now known in meditation circles as their "inner landscape". For example, a child's image of a mermaid in a drawing or story comes from real life perceptions of women and fish. Or, when writing a story a child draws on real objects but creates new situations. So, the more extensive children's experiences and perceptions are, the richer their inner landscape, the more material they have to draw on in their creative endeavours.

Vygotsky's "first and most important law" relating to imagination stated that:

> ...the creative activity of the imagination depends directly on the richness and variety of a person's previous experience because this experience provides the material from which the products of fantasy are constructed. The richer a person's experience, the richer is the material his imagination has access to.[90]

> The implication of this for education is that, if we want to build a relatively strong foundation for a child's creativity, what we must do is broaden the experiences we provide him with. All else being equal, *the more a child sees, hears, and experiences, the more he knows and assimilates, the more elements of reality he will have in his experience, and the more productive will be the operation of his imagination* (my italics).[91]

Imagination has a major role to play in the learning process because it is through our imagination that we can make sense of new information that we may not have witnessed, or new factual knowledge that we are able to imagine, drawing on what we already know. So our imagination is based on our direct experiences and our experiences feed our imagination and new learning.

Vygotsky was very interested in the notion of emotion as being a stimulating factor in learning and in imagination. Our imagination is motivated by our emotions because "... Nothing important is achieved in life without a great deal of emotion".[92] He proposed that emotions affect our imagination and vice versa. Citing the French psychologist Ribot, Vygotsky quotes, "every construct of the imagination has an effect on our feelings" whether or not the construct corresponds to reality.[93] He used the example of a child being terrified by the vision of clothes on a hanger which they imagine to be a robber. The illusion of the robber is not real but it is nonetheless terrifying. He suggests that emotions are evoked by every creative work of art, explaining why artistic creations affect us emotionally.

His final point on the relationship between reality and imagination is that a construct that arises through the imagination, such as a technical device or machine, is developed through human creativity. Once created, it has a real material form and can then impact on the environment. These creations then progress to inspire new creations.

In his study of imagination and childhood, Vygotsky was particularly interested in the study of adolescents. Adolescence is a period of change, physically, mentally and emotionally. Physiological change and the development of sexuality has a mental impact. The now more mature child develops more objective faculties, is more critical of their drawings, and starts to lose interest in childhood games and play. Vygotsky suggested that the main outlet for their creativity at this age is literary, providing a subjective outlet, while at the same time their objective reasoning faculties are developing.

> As maturity is approached, the imagination also matures, and in the transitional period between childhood and adulthood—in adolescence, starting at the time of puberty—we observe a powerful enhancement of the imagination combined with the rudiments of mature fantasy.[94]

He distinguished between imagination that is stimulated by external, observed or "plastic" impressions and that which is stimulated by "internal" thoughts or emotions. Plastic imagination is therefore objective, while emotional imagination is subjective, dependent on an individual's thoughts. Both are typical of adolescence, when "escape into an imagined world often distracts the focus and efforts of the adolescent from the real world".[95]

On the other hand the driving force of creativity is the wish to make reality out of fantasy: "Every product of the imagination, stemming from reality, attempts to complete a full circle and to be embodied in reality".[96] In adolescence young people experience dreaminess at one end of the imagination spectrum, which does not result in a creative product, while truly creative imagination involves the creation of a product, scientific, technical, literary or artistic for the adolescent and for others. This can impact on the creator's thoughts and behaviours, and future development.

Play

Playing is the child's first opportunity to develop their creativity and plays an important role in their mental, physical and emotional development. In play, a child who pretends to be a parent or to be riding a horse creates a new action or experience based on what they have already seen. Vygotsky considered play to be the "highest level of pre-school development", creating a zone of proximal development because of the way the child reworks what they have seen in real life.[97]

The *Notebooks* show that around the time of writing his lecture in 1933/4 he was rooting his theories about the playing child in the ideas of Marx and Engels. He looked at Marx's comments, noting "the crippling of development + the method of raising fully developed human beings".[98] Marx had written in *Capital* of the importance of educating children "for productive labour with instruction and gymnastics" to produce "fully developed human beings".[99] In other words children, and indeed society, need children who are all-rounders, with a breadth of educational and physical skills.

In the 1933 Leningrad Institute lecture Vygotsky said that he wanted to investigate the role of play in the pre-schooler's development to look at "first, how play itself arises in development—its origin and genesis; second, the role of this developmental activity".[100] Like his contemporary, Jean Piaget, he saw the child as progressing through stages, from toddlers under three, pre-schoolers aged three to five, school children and adolescents. This staging correlates with the child's language development, which as we have seen in the previous chapters, increasingly becomes a tool for thinking. It also correlates with their physical development which has a particularly significant impact on the thought processes of adolescents.

He was also interested in what motivates a child to play, an aspect that differentiated him from other theorists at the time. He thought that it was important that we should look at the child's "needs, inclinations, incentives and motives to act" all of which change as the infant moves towards school age. A child under three years of age wants immediate gratification, whereas the older child has developed the ability to delay gratification.

Rules and play

In this lecture he focused on pre-school children, rather than toddlers or primary-aged children because play is more significant at this age. While at play, the three-to-four year old is able to create new situations from ones that they have observed in real life, whereas the toddler simply plays with an object without being able to mentally transform it into something else. In contrast, in adolescence, imagination has progressed so that we can consider it as "play without action" because it is internalised in the mind, whereas for the younger child, play allows them to create imaginary situations while actively playing.

Vygotsky gave the example of youngsters playing at being sisters. "The elder, holding the younger by the hand, keeps telling them about other people: 'That is theirs not ours.' This means: 'My sister and I act the same, we are treated the same, but others are treated differently'. Here the emphasis is on the sameness of everything that is concentrated in the child's concept of a sister, and this means that my sister stands in a different relationship to me than other people. *What passes unnoticed by the child in real life becomes a rule in play* (my italics)". [101]

Play provides the older pre-school child with the opportunity to relate what happens in play with the norms in the real world. For example, through playing child/parent roles the child has to imagine a situation, using norms about how parents and children relate. They can then apply this understanding to their behaviour in real-life situations. In this way experimental play enables the three-to-five year old to understand the outcome of their behaviour; they are able to generalise these "affective" reactions.

So by placing themselves in this make-believe situation they become explicitly aware of the norms or "rules" of behaviour in family relationships by generalising their own experience into a game. Similarly when playing with a doll, the parent-child relationship and rules of behaviour are invoked. It is only actions that accord with the rules of the situation being enacted that are acceptable. The rules are deployed throughout the game. Where children are playing a game that has rules that govern what actions can be taken, this is in itself an imaginary situation. So Vygotsky concluded that "all games with imaginary situations are simultaneously games with rules, *and vice versa*".[102]

Play enables children to develop an awareness of social norms around them, such as behaviour at meal times, or how to relate within the family. It also allows children to construct their own rules.

Vygotsky referred to important work that Jean Piaget had written in 1932, a year before Vygotsky's Leningrad lecture, about how the child developed moral rules or boundaries of behaviour through games, learnt through interaction with adults and other children.[103] Piaget distinguished between the rules imposed on them by adults—for example, behaviour at the meal table—and the rules that children collaborate in establishing, such as how they think they should behave in a particular game. Piaget had called the situation "moral realism", when a child begins to understand what is and is not allowed, as opposed to what is possible or not on a physical level, such as not being able to light a match twice, and not being allowed to play with matches. These are external "don't" rules, established within the child's environment, whereas the child creates their own rules for a successful game.

Vygotsky's observations and experiments showed that toddlers need the actual visible presence of things and actions to make sense of things. In non-play situations the under-three year old reacts to objects according to the nature of the object. She opens and closes the door, or runs up the stairs. This is due to the thing's "motivating force"—the child's actions relate to the nature of the object that seems to demand action. In this way toddlers see objects as a stimulus for activity. So a toddler's actions are shaped by what they perceive, in combination with the effect they have on them. This union of perception, affect and motor activity impacts on how a child perceives their world or their consciousness. It also explains how a child's environment shapes their consciousness, and reinforces the importance of stimulating surroundings.

In a pre-schooler's play the object has a different role. Instead of the intrinsic nature of the object having the "motivational force", the object itself has a different, representative role allocated to it by the child. At this stage of playing, the three-to-five year old is able to be free from the constraints of the situation, and because the child starts to be imaginative, meaning starts to take precedence. He gave the example of how for pre-school children a piece of wood can represent a horse or doll and the child creates imaginary situations with this object. Ideas determine the child's action rather than the actual object, which becomes a "pivot" for making meaning —the piece of wood becomes the pivot for transferring the meaning of "horse" from the visible object horse, thereby "one of the basic psychological structures determining the child's relationship to reality is radically altered". In other words, the child is able to make their own meanings with the use of an object. This notion of "pivot" is useful in terms of understanding semiosis: words are spoken or written representations of meanings, while at this early age, pivots in the child's play represent objects.

At this stage the child is able to see their world in terms of sense and meaning, not just what they perceive. The child is perceiving things generally—a clock is not just a specific clock. The stick representing the horse ceases to be a stick, but a pivot for the meaning of the concept of a horse. But for a child, not anything can represent a horse. A postcard cannot represent a horse. The stick has properties that align with those of a horse, whereas for an adult we can suppose that any object might represent a horse because it becomes a symbol or sign for one. But for the child the stick is not a sign or symbol; this is play, where the essential features of a horse are retained, while the meaning is the main point, and the child plays with the stick as if it were a sort of horse. The use of the pivot, the wooden stick, is essential for abstracting the meaning of the word horse.

This is important because using a pivot in play enables the child to extract the meaning from an object. This sort of imaginary play is a transition between playing with real objects and thinking in abstract situations. It frees the child from the constraints of a real situation, while being subordinated to the rules of the play, and is usually seen as a pleasurable activity. This rule-governed play means that the child's actions are not impulsive. Similarly in athletic games which are necessarily imbued with rules, such as "ready, steady, go" the child cannot act impulsively but follows the rules inherent in the game. The rules make the game, which gives the child pleasure, over-riding non-rule orientated impulses.[104]

In pre-school play, it is what the actions represent, the meaning behind them that is significant. It determines what the child will do. By thinking about what they want to achieve, they act. Vygotsky described thinking as "internal action" and physical action as "external". He said that:

The child in wishing, carries out his wishes; and in thinking, he acts. Internal and external action are inseparable: imagination, interpretations, and will are internal processes in external action.[105]

Action is secondary to meaning and will. The action itself becomes the pivot for expressing an intention—so a child might stamp their feet, imagining that they are riding. It is the notion of riding that dominates their actions. Play involves "... not simply a reproduction of what he has experienced, but a creative reworking of the impressions he has acquired. He combines them and uses them to construct a new reality, one that conforms to his own needs and desires".[106]

Play creates opportunities for the child to go beyond their current perceived abilities. The "internal" or thought processes that play promotes in terms of creating a wide range of opportunities for meaning-making through imagination means that play becomes a:

...source of development and creates the zone of proximal development. Action in the imaginative sphere, in an imaginary situation, the creation of voluntary intentions, and the formation of real-life plans and volitional motives—all appear in play and make it the highest level of pre-school development.[107]

And further:

...play (also) creates the zone of proximal development of the child. In play a child is always above his average age, above his daily behaviour; in play it is as though he were a head taller than himself. As in the focus of a magnifying glass, play contains all developmental tendencies in a condensed form; in play it is as though the child were trying to jump above the level of his normal behaviour.[108]

Role-play and drama

We have seen that imitation of people and things around them is one of the features of creative play that children perform from a young age and that when children role-play their understanding of their world is enhanced. Vygotsky also showed that the act of playing allows children to create a different reality. For example, when children play at mummies and daddies, they create characters based on their impressions of what they have seen, and in doing so create a new reality. Not only is this re-enactment fun for the child, Vygotsky suggests that it is also an introduction into dramatisation. He wrote:

> Drama, more than any other form of creation, is closely and directly linked to play, which is the root of all creativity in children. Thus, drama is the most syncretic mode of creation, that is, it contains elements of the most diverse forms of creativity.[109]

Vygotsky considered that encouraging older children to put on plays tapped into and developed a wide range of creative elements. Children can write or improvise a play, as well as act, construct the set, make costumes and so on. In order to do this they need to engage with the characters and meanings within the play. He advised that children write the plays themselves because such products would be closer to their understandings than works by others. So the creative processes involved in producing a play involve technical as well as verbal and artistic skills. The value of drama for children lies with the variety of creative processes involved in developing the end product.

Learning to write through play

Vygotsky described written language as "a particular system of symbols and signs whose mastery heralds a critical turning-point in the entire cultural development of the child".[110] He described written language as being "second-order symbolism", since the system of signs that represent the sounds and words of spoken language are initially simply understood in terms of signs—letters and symbols—and gradually become real entities, understood in terms of what the signs represent. Having learnt the mechanical process of how to form letters, learning to write, like learning to read, should be taught in terms of written language, as apart from an abstract system of sounds and letters divorced from meaning.

Vygotsky suggested that the earliest forms of writing take place through the simple gestures children make, "writing in the air", which stand for or symbolise an intention. "The gesture is the initial visual sign that contains the child's future as an acorn contains a future oak."[111] Children's scribbles are also early forms of writing. The child has started to use semiotic representation, making meaning through signs, through gestures or simple scribbles that are representative of meanings in a similar way to letters and words representing meanings.

These early scribbles and gestures can be seen as "first order" symbols because they are intended to directly represent objects or actions. The child can "read" them back to an adult. So these symbols also act as mnemonics, reminding the child of their intentions and meanings that they are creating. This is an important early function of the written word. The role of the teacher in this context is to "shift the child's activity from drawing things to drawing speech".[112] Ultimately the child will perceive written language in the same way as they perceive speech.

So make-believe play and drawing play a key role in the development of a child's thinking process and in the development of writing. Vygotsky stresses the importance of making this learning fun, through the use of games and meaningful situations, and most importantly making literacy "necessary for something", something the child needs for communication. It is a "complex cultural activity" so should not be taught purely as a motor skill. It should be seen as a "natural activity" and not as "training from without".[113] The writers of the materials and curriculum used to teach "Literacy" in most UK primary schools should read this work!

Children's creative writing

Vygotsky also explored play and writing in an extensive article he wrote on imagination, written before the Leningrad Pedagogical Institute lecture on play. *Imagination and Creativity in Childhood* was an extensive study, analysing the different creative activities in which children use their imagination.[114] In addition to play and writing, he looked at story writing, drawing and technology. This article shows his particular interest in children's creative writing.[115]

Children are familiar with spoken language being used in a communicative context since it is an everyday personal experience. But writing has its own rules that differ from those used in speaking:

> When he begins to switch to written language, which is vastly more abstract and arbitrary, the child often does not understand what he should write. He does not have any intrinsic motivation to write.[116]

This is why the writing of children is less mature than their oracy, their ability to express themselves fluently and grammatically through speech. It is also the reason that children need to be explicitly taught the conventions of writing. But the texts that children are asked to write should be relevant to their lives. He drew substantially on Tolstoy's ideas and experience of working with children and their story making. Tolstoy was critical of teaching methods that made children write from a selection of topics, with only rudimentary writing guidelines, rather than explaining why they should write and the use of their writing. Tolstoy believed that this lack of explicit guidance meant that "they did not understand the art—the beauty of expressing life in words and the attraction of this art".[117] Vygotsky adds that the child's literary creativity would be enhanced if they were emotionally engaged in the topic, and encouraged to express their "interior world in words".[118]

Vygotsky respected Tolstoy's description of the excitement

that can be generated through literary creation, and his conclusion that "the true task of education is not to prematurely inculcate adult language in children, but to help the child develop and shape his own literary language". [119] Vygotsky was optimistic about the possible role of education in children's literary development and was critical of Tolstoy's negative approach to education and his idealisation of childhood. For Vygotsky, the point of education was development for the future, for both the child's future and the revolutionary state's future.

Vygotsky was influenced by the work of Blonsky, colleague, comrade and former lecturer. Blonsky discussed the need to motivate children in literary education through teaching genres and styles that were relevant to them, rather than the more formal unfamiliar traditional literary styles. Vygotsky wrote:

> The teachers who thus incorrectly guided their pupils' literary creativity often killed the spontaneous beauty, individuality, and vitality of children's language and impeded their mastery of written language as a special way of expressing one's thoughts and feelings. Instead, the children developed, to use Blonsky's expression, the type of school jargon that is produced by the purely mechanical inculcation of children with the artificial bookish language of adults. [120]

Vygotsky agreed with Tolstoy that children should always know about the topics they are given to write about, and should have thought about these topics deeply. Blonsky had suggested that the best genres for children were notes, letters to real people and very short stories. Letters were a common form of communication and would therefore engage children, as well as being educative and useful. This would also be motivational for children.

But it is adolescents' writing that was of most interest to Vygotsky. Adolescents no longer play, they are no longer so interested in drawing, unless they are particularly talented, but they do write. Childish behaviour and interests wane, and the now more experienced teenager develops reasoning and creative faculties that are akin to adult thinking. In the 1931 article on imagination he drew attention to the writing of adolescents because he thought that creative writing was the main means through which imagination is developed, and is an outlet for the maturing teenager.

As the child grows into an adolescent, increasing sexualisation shatters the equilibrium of childhood, so the adolescent seeks a new equilibrium.

> A whole new world of inner experiences, urges, and attractions opens up at this age; the child's inner life becomes infinitely more complex compared to that in the earlier years of childhood. His relationships to those around him and to his environment become vastly more complex; the impressions he receives from the external world undergo more profound processing.[121]

This change of physical and mental state means that the adolescent creates an "internal crisis" and so they become more emotional and emotionally volatile, creating the ideal state of mind for creative writing. They can use language to express their inner thoughts and deal with increasingly complex relationships. The discarding of childish drawing in favour of writing reflects the deeper and perhaps troubled thinking of the adolescent. It also correlates with the development of abstract thought. Creative writing plays a major role in developing language and therefore thinking skills.

> Its significance lies in the fact that it deepens, expands, and purifies the child's emotional life, which for the first time is awakened and tuned to a serious key. Finally, it is important because it permits the child, by exercising his creative tendencies and skills, to master human language, this extremely subtle and complex tool for

forming and expressing human thoughts, human feelings, and the human inner world.[122]

Conclusion

Vygotsky was committed to developing teachers who would
provide creative and enjoyable opportunities for their students,
and to the development of Russian education that would
provide a range of learning experiences. His studies showed
the importance of providing school pupils with enriching
experiences which give them the material for their creativity
and therefore their thinking and learning. He said: "The right
kind of education involves awakening in the child what already
exists within him, helping him to develop it and directing this
development in a particular direction".[123]

Some people have interpreted Vygotsky's work on play
to mean that all learning should be play-based, child-centred
and exploratory. This was not what Vygotsky was getting at.
He thought that schools and youth groups should promote
opportunities for creativity, on the one hand, but where
academic concepts are necessary for learning these need to be
explicitly taught within pupils' zones of proximal development.
He thought this was also true of some aspects of formal writing
so that children understand the literary demands of the task.

His work on imagination demonstrates how important it is
to look at the processes involved in learning, to understand the
roots of learning, language and thinking, and to consider the
challenges faced by students and the importance of making the
action of learning engaging and motivational.

Vygotsky showed us that the importance of the promotion
of imagination across the curriculum, across the arts, sciences
and technologies is essential.

> The entire future of humanity will be attained through
> the creative imagination; orientation to the future,
> behaviour based on the future and derived from
> this future, is the most important function of the

imagination. To the extent that the main educational objective of teaching is guidance of school children's behavior so as to prepare them for the future, development and exercise of the imagination should be one of the main forces enlisted for the attainment of this goal. The development of a creative individual, one who strives for the future, is enabled by creative imagination embodied in the present.[124]

Chapter 7
Special Educational Needs &
Disability and Defectology

Vygotsky's work with children with a range of learning and emotional challenges took place in the context of the aftermath of the October Revolution of 1917 and the Civil War that followed it. Despite the positive political outcomes of the Revolution, some of the effects of the massive political upheaval meant that there were many children who were malnourished, orphaned, or homeless, many who had lost out on education, and some who were mentally and physically traumatised and damaged.

When the new Soviet education departments were established, many of the problems still existed but there was a significant development in the educational provision for these children. The new medical, educational and psychological study of special needs was known as "Defectology", which mainly referred to deaf-mute and autistic children. Vygotsky played a highly influential role in this new discipline, where he became the founder of a cultural-historical method.

We should note that many of the terms used in the Soviet Union at this time in the context of special needs, translated as "abnormal", "retarded" or "handicapped" child and "defectology", do not sit well in the context of our current understanding of Special Educational Needs and Disability (SEND). They appear to be negative. The terms reflect the period in which he was working and were not intended to be negatively discriminatory. Vygotsky's attitude to the range of children in these categories was positive. He considered that the "defect" in the child does not cause them to have a "defective" personality, but that we should understand such children as having a different process of development.

> A child whose development is impeded by a defect is not simply a child less developed than his peers; rather he has developed differently... a child in each stage of his development, in each of his phases, represents a qualitative uniqueness, ie a specific organic and psychological structure; in precisely the same way a handicapped child represents a qualitatively different, unique type of development.[125]

As a teacher-trainer in Gomel in 1917, Vygotsky taught his trainees about special educational needs. But his clinical practice with children with a range of challenging special needs started in 1924 when he become involved in the work of the Section for Abnormal Children in the People's Commissariat of Education and played a leading role in the Congress for the Struggle against Child Defectiveness, Homelessness and Delinquency which was set up by the government to address the dreadful circumstances of some of these children. The children he treated and studied had a variety of mental health challenges and physical disabilities—deaf-mute, blind, and some had learning difficulties. He also worked with adults who were diagnosed with schizophrenia and Alzheimer's Disease.[126]

Vygotsky worked both as a practitioner and researcher at specialist SEND institutes. He was seen by others in the field as an expert, a consultant, and used to preside over weekly discussions and presentations of interesting cases with a collective of psychiatrists, psychologists, educationalists and students. Despite this high esteem, after his death in 1936, discussion of his work was prohibited in the Great Purge of

Stalin's Soviet Union, which banned "paedology", the study of children's mental, social and physical development, in preference to a behaviourist psychology. Their special schools were separated from SEND research institutions.

Vygotsky's innovational theory and practice in this field was at the heart of his commitment to the creation of a dialectical materialist psychology. In 1929, the government was starting to attempt to split research from practice in psychology; keen to create a positive dynamic experience for SEND pupils, based on cultural-historical and holistic principles, Vygotsky wrote in *The Fundamental Problems of Defectology*:[127]

> ...defectology faces tasks the solution of which demand creative work and the introduction of special forms. To solve these and other problems of defectology it is necessary to find a solid foundation for both theory and practice. In order not to build on sand, to avoid the eclectic and superficial empiricism which characterised it in the past, in order to shift away from a clinical-therapeutic approach to a positive, creative pedagogy, defectology must rest on the same dialectic and materialist foundation and be guided by our pedagogy in general, that is, by the social foundation which determines our social education. [128]

Prior to the new defectology movement, traditional approaches to special needs were mainly test-based: "In defectology, counting and measuring came before experimentation, observation, analysis, generalisation, description, and qualitative diagnosis".[129] Such methods look at "yesterday's development" and do not allow for individual social strengths or experiences.

Throughout his life Vygotsky drew on his work with children with disabilities to develop his general psychological and paedological theories. Despite his extensive clinical work with children with a range of special needs, most of his published work on defectology relates to theoretical principles, apart from clinical notes in his Notebooks.

Perspectives on defectology

Vygotsky's studies and practice in defectology continued for the rest of his life. During that time his focus was two-fold: an analysis of the *physical* or *psychological* problem presented and, more importantly to him, a focus on the *social, emotional and developmenta*l impact of the disability on the pupil or adult and how appropriate interaction and instruction can aid the child's development. On the medical side he also studied the impact that these experiences had on the brain and the child's endocrine systems.

He was committed to the Pioneer programme, equivalent to the Scout movement, for nine to 15 year olds, but including sporting activities as a way to increase the child's self image, as an equalising, engaging and useful means of integrating young people with a range of special needs, as well as providing extensive practical learning and sporting opportunities.

He had an optimistic view of development for each SEND child. His theoretical and practical work in SEND incorporated his theories of children's cognitive development, the zone of proximal development, developmental education, as well as the vital role of mediation in learning, and the importance of the social and cultural situation. Unlike the prevailing deficit-oriented models of disablement during his time, Vygotsky regarded children with special educational needs in positive terms. He thought that a disabled child should not be perceived, primarily, in terms of their disability, but as a "normal" person who may well have exceptional talents. This perspective underpinned Vygotsky's attitudes to research and practical work with SEND children.

In line with his other psychological work, he was interested in the *ontogenesis*—the sociocultural and historical development—of the SEND child and how they differed from "normal" children. Broadly speaking, Vygotsky analysed two categories of children with SEND—those who were physically or sensorily impaired and those who were "mentally retarded", whom we would now describe as having "learning difficulties". In his study of children with learning difficulties, he sub-divided two broad groups: those whose problems stemmed from physiological circumstances and those who became underdeveloped, and hence socially delayed, due to adverse environmental factors in their lives or at school.[130] Both may display similar phenomena.

While recognising that learning difficulties might be physiologically caused, that is through problems at childbirth, or genetic disorders, he thought that SEND children, particularly deaf-mute students, had emotional challenges relating to their social experiences, because of the way people related to them and the way they perceived themselves. Focusing on the social environmental factors that affect the development of these children, he believed that their under-development or "retardation" stemmed from the difficult conditions they experienced at home or at school. In addition, the attitudes of the family, which too often tended to treat their children as defective, that is, as a disabled rather than a "normal" person, may have had negative outcomes. Changing attitudes and conditions in the home could positively impact on SEND children, increasing their own self-image and hence enabling many previously "uneducatable" or "unmanageable" children to thrive. The effect of this sort of compensatory approach can then counteract the social conditions that caused the original difficulties.

One of the main reasons for this different sort of development is due to the way that other people interact with the child with special needs. They are seen as different, and therefore treated differently:

> Any physical handicap, be it deafness, blindness
> or inherent mental retardation, not only changes
> a person's attitude toward the world, but first and
> foremost affects his relationship with people. Any

physical defect, or flaw, is conceived as a behavioural abnormality. Even within his or her family, a deaf or blind child is first of all a special child, toward whom one develops an exclusive, unusual attitude, which is different from that toward other children.[131]

This negative or over-protective attitude towards the deaf-mute child can lead to *disontogenesis*, when the child's development becomes distorted by the prevailing environment.

Vygotsky was impressed by Adler's theories which looked at the potential of SEND children and how they establish their own mechanism for dealing with their disability: they develop natural tendencies to compensate for their areas of weakness. Using Marxist terminology (by referring to "superstructure") he wrote:

What a liberating truth for the pedagogue! A blind child develops a psychological superstructure circum-venting his impaired vision with only one goal in mind: to replace sight. Using every possible means available to him, a deaf child works out ways to overcome the isolation and seclusion caused by his deafness. Up to now we have neglected these psychological powers. We have not taken into account the desire with which such a child struggles to be healthy and fully accepted socially. A defect has been statically viewed as merely a defect, a minus. Education has neglected the positive forces created by a defect.[132]

Thus the particular handicap of the individual child often meant that this child compensated for the handicap by developing strengths in their other senses. He wrote of the deaf and blind American socialist, Helen Keller and how her double sensory impairment motivated her to overcome her disability: "...her defect did not become a brake but was transformed into a drive which insured her development".[133] This "overcompensation" is determined by two factors—the extent of the disability and by the "compensatory reserve and the wealth and diversity of functions" which the child possesses.[134] Of course in Helen Keller's case, in addition to her family wealth, she had a dedicated tutor who became her lifelong friend, who initially taught her to communicate through sign language and how to speak through feeling throat vibrations—two invaluable cultural tools for the mediation of communication and thinking.

Vygotsky applied his optimistic ZPD theory to his interpretation of the development of SEND children, stressing the importance of recognising their developmental potential:

> The world pours, through a large funnel as it were, in thousands of stimuli, drives and callings; inside from the narrow end as response reactions of the organism in greatly reduced quantity. The actualised behaviour is but an infinitesimal part of the possible behaviour. Man is full of unrealised opportunities at any given moment. These unrealised opportunities for behaviour, the disparity between the broad and narrow ends of the funnel, is an indisputable reality, just as real as the reactions that have prevailed.[135]

Teaching hearing-impaired and mute children

When Vygotsky travelled to London in 1925, he presented a paper, on behalf of the Commissariat, at an International Conference on the Education of the Deaf held in what is now the Institute of Education, part of University College, London.[136] The paper was entitled "Principles of Social Education for Deaf and Dumb Children in Russia". This paper addressed his general psychological theory and his proposals relating to the education of deaf and mute children in the context of Revolutionary Soviet Union education. A central thrust in this talk was that despite deafness being a physical disability, this impairment creates a "social sprain" and the teacher needs to deal with the social impact of the disability. "Blindness or deafness, as a psychological fact, is not at all a misfortune, but as a social fact, it becomes such".[137] So it is important that they are not isolated from other children and are specifically helped to communicate with others and to develop positive self-images.

Even at this early stage in his research and practice, Vygotsky recognised the vital role that language has to play in thinking processes and therefore focussed on the importance of teaching deaf children to talk, for their cognitive development. "Speech does not only serve as a means of intercourse between children, but also as an instrument of thought."[138] He was concerned that young pre-school deaf children would not have access to hearing speech and therefore not able to learn to use language in the same way as non-impaired children. His solution for deaf children was to place them in pre-schools where they were explicitly taught the rudiments of speaking so that they could develop logical speech. He was adamant that they should be taught to hear and speak in a natural and positive way, so that speech was seen as "necessary and interesting".[139] They needed to be able to chatter, to use language functionally, but they also needed to learn the rudiments of using the voice and making sounds, and of lip-reading, which they practised daily for two hours.

Vygotsky proposed that the schooling of hearing-impaired children should proceed along similar principles used in pre-school education. He criticised the old "dead" methods of focussing on sounds instead of meaning, context, sense, that were still used in schools, so now "...it is the fight for a whole word, an intelligent sentence, a logical, natural speech" that teachers of the deaf should pursue.[140] Teaching should be focussing on the use of logical language, whole words and sentences, not on fragments of sound. Breaking words down into sounds makes them meaningless and takes away their role in thinking. It is through this meanings-based method that children can learn aspects of sounds and speaking, as well as thinking. He proposed a multi-sensory approach which was visual and motor-based; lip-reading, "reading from the face", underpinned everything, but in addition "reading" images of words on the speaker's lips, or words on the blackboards, and moving the hand in writing. "The problem is, so to speak, to 'throw' the deaf and dumb into our speech, with the result that the child goes mechanically into logical speech without special effort."[141] All the words taught were in sentences or phrases, and in a relevant context, for example "Children sit down" or "Children go to your seats".

He compared this method of teaching relevant language, which was based on engaging deaf and mute children in wanting and needing to speak, and using speech as a logical meaning-making process, with the method used by the traditional school which destroys children's motivation and…

> …which separates the deaf and dumb child from normal surroundings and places it in a special environment, where everything is adapted to its infirmities; thus, the circle of its interests becomes very narrow and this encourages unsociable instincts.[142]

He went on to explain that education for all in the Russian Socialist Federative Soviet Republic was geared towards a "labour education", where school is seen as a part of normal social life. Education was seen to be part of society, for society and through society. Deaf and mute children were educated under the same principle. They should be "Pioneers", participating in games with other non-impaired children, and they need to be directly engaged, not bystanders. Vygotsky ended this talk with a passionate speech praising the People's Education and the challenges and achievements of the Revolution.

It is interesting to note that although this talk took place early in his career when he already had a depth of analysis of the needs of deaf and mute children, as well as the educational framework in the new USSR, some of his analysis about their learning was reflexological. For example, he wrote that children need to repeatedly practise saying words so that they are learned as a reflex. Later he recognised the mediated meaning-making processes involved in speaking and literacy.

Despite the Stalinist regime's dismissive attack on defectology and on Vygotsky's work, his Institute of Defectology ran schools for the deaf, which continued for many years after his death, following Vygotsky's pedological and pedagogical principles. The BBC made a documentary, The Butterflies of Zagorsk, which shows how one of the Institute's schools in Zagorsk, 40 miles from Moscow, was working in the 1970s with young partially sighted and partially hearing secondary-aged pupils.[143] Some arrived at the school in a traumatised state but were reassured by the one-to-one work with teachers. Every child was taught to communicate through finger-spelling, sign language and the use of vibration. There was great pride in this school. Pupils graduated from the school into university courses.

Work with emotionally-disturbed children

Vygotsky practised as a psychiatrist, with emotionally-disturbed children and with adults diagnosed with schizophrenia and Alzheimer's Disease. It should be remembered that there was very little if any mental health medication at this time. His notes about working with disturbed children show that the approach was multidisciplinary, and included a psychodynamic analysis, which was quite popular at the time, although it was not in accord with Stalinist behaviourist principles.

Vygotsky was interested in Freud's work, whose psychology was social, rather than biological. In his PhD thesis, The Psychology of Art, he had showed a particular interest in the analysis of the impact of death in Freud's Beyond the Pleasure Principle, analysing Hamlet in psychodynamic terms. (He thought that art, and literature in this case, protected the artist when discussing rape and murder, because it is fantasy.) We can see from his case notes that he applied psychodynamic interpretations to his patients.

In 1933-4 Vygotsky worked with disturbed children as a clinical psychologist in the Donskaya Clinic, part of the Pirogov

Second Moscow Medical Institute. Fifteen years after the 1917 Revolution, and five years after the Stalinist counter-revolution, there was still dreadful poverty, abuse and homelessness. His clinical records of 36 of the children he saw at the clinic, published in his *Notebooks*, show his methodology in practice.[144] These notes detail the social, physical, medical and educational problems displayed by the child, the history, or *ontogenesis* of the symptoms, as well as details of their parents' social and psychological issues. The narratives are traumatic, with stories of violent parents, parental alcohol abuse, homelessness and sexual jealousies between daughter and mother relating to stepfathers. It is interesting to observe Vygotsky's multidisciplinary approach, with evident Freudian interpretations.

One particularly disturbing case concerned a boy who had witnessed his cousin being run over and killed by a car. His cousin's father, his uncle, had accused the boy of the death. The boy was deeply traumatised by what he had seen. Vygotsky's notes are socially, educationally and medically detailed. The boy had had poor grades in school, but had been a popular student. After the accident he started to have serious difficulties with eating, becoming phobic about food, and he had nightmares and hallucinations. He developed a limp in the same leg his cousin had had crushed in the accident. Vygotsky took notes of the boy's concerns and dreams, recorded that his grandfather was an alcoholic and his aunt and mother were epileptics. His mother had had nine pregnancies and three abortions and a child who had died of meningitis. The boy had suffered from whooping cough and scarlet fever. His father, whom Vygotsky described as having a pathological personality, was a drinker.

Vygotsky observed the boy's interactions with the other children in the hospital where he was quiet, but friendly. He recounted the boy's retelling of events, and observed his limp. He concluded that the boy had an anxiety about death to which the food phobia was related because of what Vygotsky suggested were his cannibalistic thoughts; the food anxiety related to these cannibalistic thoughts that he was eating his cousin's flesh. While the boy had suffered from delusions—the pain in his legs, auditory and visual hallucinations and misinterpretations of events, he did not necessarily consider him to have schizophrenia but to have reactions to the traumatic events.

> The centre of the delusion is the identification with the deceased cousin (through the pains in his legs). The positive of reality are the threats: the negative is the suicidal tendency: I should have died... He sees his uncle with a knife (his own death) in the plate with meat.[145]

This case study shows how rigorous Vygotsky was in his work. His note of the illnesses was not to specifically medicalise the boy's problems, although they may have highlighted physiological vulnerabilities, but to show the physical, social and historical environment in which the child had grown up, which could have impacted on his psychological well-being. His analysis shows the influence of Freudian theories, which Vygotsky had incorporated into his dialectical materialist psychology since psychodynamic theory is a social theory of behaviour.

Vygotsky also worked with adults who were diagnosed with schizophrenia. Most of the surviving articles relate to interpretations of their language and thinking processes. It should be noted that of course there were then no specific antipsychotic medications for people with this diagnosis.

Inclusive education and specialist schooling

In Vygotsky's time, special schools had been run by educators, still influenced by the old "bourgeois mentality" of the western world, inspired by religious or philanthropic notions of feeling pity for these children, who were seen as a burden. Vygotsky argued that a revolutionary and scientific approach would be one that integrated these children into mainstream schooling, allowing them to be taught alongside their "normal" peers and hence enable them to feel like other Russian children. In this way, blind and deaf children would be able to see and hear, in a metaphorical sense, and would perceive themselves and their world as other children do. He wrote of the old-fashioned SEND education in Russia:

> There's not a grain of stoicism in the traditional education of children with mental defects. This education has been weakened by a tendency toward pity and philanthropy; it has been poisoned by morbidness and sickliness. Our education is insipid; it nips the pupil in the bud; there is no salt to this education. We need tempered and courageous ideas. Our ideal is not to cover over a sore place with cotton wadding and protect it with various methods from further bruises but to clear a wide path for overcoming the defect, for overcompensation.[146]

Throughout the period that he was working in the Soviet Union, the care and education of SEND children was divided between the "curative" schools run by the Soviet Ministry of Health, which catered for children with severe health (eg cerebral palsy) or psychiatric (eg autism) problems, and the Soviet Ministry of Education, which educated all other children in mainstream schools. Pupils with serious physical SENDs were educated in special residential schools.

He was critical of the teaching of "mentally retarded children" in Russian schools which focused on weaknesses and confined to methods requiring concrete rather than abstract thought, in the expectation, based on test results, that these children were incapable of abstract reasoning or thought. These methods were found to be failing the children whose disabilities were reinforced because they were acclimatised to thinking only on the concrete level, and whose thinking failed to progress on the abstract level.

Vygotsky was committed to the provision of an education system that developed every child to their full capacity. He stressed that it is particularly important for teachers of children with learning difficulties to be sensitive to the learning needs of their students and give them scaffolded teaching strategies to enable them to develop their potential. He advised that, when left to themselves, these children will never:

> ...achieve well-elaborated forms of abstract thought, the school should make every effort to push them in that direction and to develop in them what is intrinsically lacking in their own development... Concreteness is... necessary and unavoidable only as a stepping stone for developing abstract thinking—as a means and not an end in itself.[147]

As we have seen, he believed that prioritising socialisation for SEND children was essential. "Social education will conquer physical handicaps".[148] Social education was essential since such children perceived their disability in social rather than psychological terms. They saw themselves as socially different, rather than as perceiving the world differently. Thus the job of special needs educators, and parents of such children, was firstly to treat these children as "normal", to focus on the child's health and strengths, rather than their weaknesses, to see the child as a "normal" human being, not as one with a particular problem or difficulty. Teachers of SEND children should not patronise them, treat them as "blind" or "deaf"; instead they should work on their strengths: "To educate a child as a blind or a deaf child means to nurture blindness and deafness; such an attitude means that the pedagogy of children with defects will become a defective pedagogy".[149]

Following Marx's proposal that games and gymnastics help to produce "fully developed human beings" Vygotsky suggested that games which include being silent could be so much more useful than insisting on silence in the passive learning classroom.[150] Vygotsky advocated the use of games that encouraged social participation. He also proposed that deaf and dumb children should become involved in the young pioneering programme run by the Deaf and Dumb Children's Communist movement. "The pioneer movement is, from a pedagogical point of view, an experiment of building and organising children's games in an international and universal spirit".[151] The games entailed in this programme relate to practical life experiences, helping to socialise the SEND child as well as developing their higher mental functions.

Vygotsky was interested in the fact that some children with learning difficulties had a specific problem with their memory, which hampered their further learning. It was therefore important that teachers were aware of the learning difficulty and its impact, and that they should provide appropriate learning "tools" for every SEND child, to facilitate their daily functioning as well as developing their higher mental functions. He was referring to psychological tools like appropriate language and teaching, and material tools like aids.

Teaching a blind child how to use finger-spelling, or a deaf child how to feel sound vibrations to develop speech would enable them to learn as effectively as the un-handicapped child. Teachers should also be aware of how children use these tools, and the processes they use in their learning. He called this "fundamental points for defining the cultural development of the abnormal child".[152] This holistic assessment would give a rounded and detailed picture of the child, exposing their strengths and areas of weakness.

Differentiation became important to Vygotsky in his later work, when he proposed that staff should be committed to meeting the individual needs of every child. But teaching should also develop those social skills through collaborative learning and a curriculum that develops imagination and play.

Vygotsky wanted to promote schooling for SEND pupils that treated them as "normal" students. He disliked the paternalistic patronisation that took place in the traditional Russian special schools:

Liberate the special school from its slavery—that is

from the physical handicap to which it has become enslaved—which only nurtures but does not cure. Liberate the special school from any trace of philanthropic and religious orientation. Rebuild it on healthy pedagogical ground. Free the child from the unbearable and senseless burden of special schooling.[153]

He was committed to the principle that educational provision for SEND pupils should be integrated with mainstream pupils, as far as possible. This was a very progressive idea at the time since SEND education had been dominated by pre-revolutionary defectologists who believed in a formalised education, dominated by drilling "teaching" strategies. Things did not change until some years after 1921, when the Commissariat of Enlightenment was set up to meet the needs of the huge numbers of abandoned and needy children. Vygotsky gave two reports to their congress and thereafter offered a significant contribution to the way in which SEND pupils were educated.

Conclusion

Vygotsky's approach was extraordinarily modern, holistic and inclusive: one that would significantly benefit those currently working with children with SEND. The teaching strategies that he proposed can be found in good special schools, but could also be used where mainstream classrooms are adequately resourced with specialist trained teachers.

In today's educational world, where children are increasingly labelled into medicalised categories, Vygotsky's ideas provide us with a deeper insight into understanding and working with a range of pupils with SEND, the importance of recognising and developing the strengths of all, encouraging social integration, as well as a further understanding of the relevance of the application of a dialectical materialist model in understanding SEND.

Chapter 8
Vygotsky's Legacy

Nearly one hundred years after his death, Vygotsky has left us with a wealth of ideas to better understand ourselves, our children, how people learn and develop and the importance of communication in thinking, doing and knowing. The most important legacy he leaves is that in order to understand what makes us tick we need to look through the lens of a social materialist analysis.

Our social history and the environment in which we have lived play a crucial role in shaping our consciousness and our learning. So the more resourceful our environment, the richer our inner landscape, the more we have to draw on to understand our world and to create new thinking and learning. Vygotsky's analysis was holistic. In addition to our social environment, our physical well-being matters. Importantly, Vygotsky also considered the biology of children. The mind is realised through the biological brain and is affected by physical factors. This dialectical relationship between our individual human biology and our social environment impacts on who we are, what we do, how we do it.

His work on speaking and thinking shows us the significance of communication and collaboration in our thinking and doing. Collaboration, whether it is between teacher/parent and child, in the street, or between working colleagues, expands thinking through inter/intramental processes. And throughout his work we understand that these processes are intrinsically social, not just because they involve people, but because they involve tools such as language or technology, which themselves are socially formed.

During Vygotsky's lifetime, Stalin failed in his attempts to split the *theory* of defectology from the *practice* of teaching children with special needs. If we want our students to reach into their zone of proximal development we need to be informed by theory, such as the mass of paedological ideas that Vygotsky has left us.

Politics strongly influenced his views on education. This is explicit in his commitment to a Marxist, revolutionary and egalitarian educational system. He was also aware of how politics, bourgeois or revolutionary, shapes the educational system. Vygotsky wrote:

> Pedagogics is never and was never politically indif-
> ferent, since willingly or unwillingly, through its own
> work on the psyche, it has always adopted a particular
> social pattern, political line, in accordance with the
> dominant social class that has guided its interests.[154]

He was driven by his political commitment to establish a Marxist psychology and to promote the best possible learning possibilities for each child, and to create a well-educated population for Revolutionary Russia. In education in the UK today there is a heavy focus on skills and knowledge sound bites, the antithesis of Vygotsky's work, and more akin to pre-revolutionary Russian educational practice. While Ofsted wants to measure classroom *practices* as *outcomes*, Vygotsky focused on *processes*. He did not see speaking as a "skill" but as a mental tool. Language is the socially constructed tool that enables us to exchange ideas, develop them through communication with others and through our own inner speech, thinking through our own thoughts. Vygotsky's intra-active/

interactive model of thinking and learning means that the best learning environments for pupils are ones that facilitate talk between children and talk between teacher and pupils.

Despite its more complex nature, writing acts as a mediational tool. We know that as we sit down to write, the process of writing helps to formulate our ideas. Similarly, computers can act as tools for mediating our thinking. For blind pupils, Braille acts as a mediational thinking tool, and for deaf children sign language plays a similar role in the thinking process.

It is currently fashionable in classrooms for teachers to identify "key words" at the start of each lesson. Vygotsky would have approved of this strategy if it meant that these are the key concepts that students need to understand by the end of the lesson or unit, because concepts are the key as to why and how language mediates thinking. They hold meanings; they also represent knowledge. The notions of *everyday* and *academic* concepts, and the different ways that these concepts are learned—one through everyday experiences, the other through explicit teaching—can help teachers to identify what it is they want their students to learn and how. At the same time, it is important for us to recognise that what is an everyday concept for one student or person, is an academic concept for another, one that needs to be explicitly taught. The more a child's or person's background resembles that of school or an academic environment, the more familiar they will be with what might be academic concepts. This means that educators need to explicitly teach their students academic concepts, and provide a breadth of experience to enable students to develop a range of academic concepts to deepen their learning. This is why it is a misunderstanding of Vygotskian pedagogy to assume that Vygotsky was promoting a "pick-up" method, one where the student learns by doing and playing; he was actually suggesting the explicit teaching of academic concepts.

In his seminal article on *Imagination and Creativity in Childhood*, Vygotsky stressed the importance of developing creativity which underpins "absolutely all aspects of cultural life, enabling artistic, scientific, and technical creation alike".[155] He demonstrated how children's imagination and creativity should be developed throughout childhood, starting with play for toddlers and continuing across the school curriculum for school students. Education should be creative and it should be fun, in order to engage learners. He identified the significance of previous experiences in creativity. We do not create from a blank canvas but draw on what we have previously perceived. So it is important that schooling provides students with enriching experiences to develop their imagination and therefore their learning achievements.

This is a very different model to that expounded by current UK government educational policy. In 1998 David Blunkett, Labour Education Secretary of State, launched a range of national strategies to "raise standards" and develop "literacy". At the heart of this was the National Literacy Strategy, which is still followed by most primary schools, who devote an hour a day to teaching "literacy skills". Literacy—mainly reading and writing—was and is seen as a set of skills. Vygotskian thinking informs us that literacy is in fact a tool for thinking and learning, a tool that relates to a context or to subject matter rather than something that stands on its own. The written and spoken language we use acts as a means of thinking through and shaping our thinking. So to test six year olds on nonsense words, where they are expected to combine letters and sounds, does not help them to learn, and teaches words as extraneous to meaning. "Words" are not being read as words, as language, as we use and know language. By removing the social context in which language is used Vygotsky would have claimed that words and the notion of "literacy" have been fetishised, isolating them from their meanings and contextual functions.

The legacy that most people who know a bit about Vygotsky refer to is the zone of proximal development. This beautiful and optimistic notion enables us to look to the potential in people. But the important element of this theory is that it is a social interactive theory, depending on the effective scaffolding by the teacher or more competent peer. The notions of *interactive* and *intra-active* thinking and learning are embedded in this idea. This helps us to understand the crucial role of communication in learning.

In today's competitive world, education is seen in terms of *standards* that students, teachers and schools are expected to meet. Governments do this by attempting to measure children's learning through Standard Assessment Tests (SATS) and examinations. Ofsted also make judgements on schools based on these test results. Vygotsky's work on the zone of proximal development shows us how tests and exams do not promote learning, but rather measure "yesterday's development".

For decades educational priorities have been framed in terms of *standards* and *skills*. Before the 1970s, reading and writing *skills* were the main focus for politicians. But in 1976 Prime Minister James Callaghan, in a speech at Ruskin College, initiated a significant change in education policy. This was the precursor to the Thatcher Education Reform Act of 1988 which brought in the National Curriculum and the rigorous testing and levelling contained in it. He introduced the notion of a core curriculum, and led an attack on *informal teaching methods* and demands for more and better *skills*. In 2014 Tory Secretary of State Michael Gove, again referring to *standards*, announced more reforms in education, including removing much of the coursework from GCSE and A levels, making them more exam-orientated.

The result of these political drives is an education system driven by standards and skills, testing children from the moment they enter schools, through to examinations when they leave. Children need to reach levels therefore teaching is increasingly orientated towards passing tests, rather than towards the process of engagement and learning.

As austerity increasingly blights people's lives, the mental health of children and adults suffers profoundly. Vygotskian thought helps us to look at the whole picture when considering the roots of mental health problems—the health and social environment of the child and their parents. He separated the notion of *brain*, the biological organ, from *mind*, that is responsible for our conscious thinking. Mental distress in all its forms occurs in the mind, but because the brain operates the nervous system we need to consider the biological as well as the social and psychological factors affecting mental health. Vygotsky's holistic approach to mental health informs us that it is important to analyse both the patient's history in terms of their social experiences and behaviours, and that of their parents, and also their biological history. This analysis helps us to understand why some people develop more psychological health problems that others—some are more vulnerable in terms of their biology. Medication to treat psychological health had not been developed in Vygotsky's day, so his treatment was mainly psychodynamic. Today, effective work with people struggling with mental health challenges could be a blend of medical, psychological and social work. The lesson that we learn from Vygotsky is to look at the breadth of factors that can cause mental health problems.

Vygotsky was a towering intellect and innovator whose philosophy of education, theories of children's development and theories and practice in psychology were the antithesis of what we are confronted with today. After nearly three decades of successive "reforms", our education and mental health systems mirror the competitive impetus of capitalist society. The testing and grading regime, the ranking of students and hospitals, wholesale privatisation, systemic inequalities, are the opposite of his vision of education and psychology that prioritises the flowering potential of every student in a society based on co-operation in a "harmonious society of equals". It is a legacy worth fighting for.

Chronology

Lev Semyonovich Vygotsky 1896-1934

1896 Vygotsky born and lived in Gomel (now Belarus) from the age of seven.

1913 Left school. Studied Medicine and then Law at University of Moscow. Studied Linguistics, Psychology and Philosophy at Shaniavsky People's University.

1915 *The Tragedy of Hamlet, Prince of Denmark* (written).

1917 Russian Revolution (February and October). Vygotsky gradated from both universities.

1919 Taught in a vocational school.

1921-1923 Also taught in a teachers' college in Gomel. Set up psychology laboratory for the study of children and adults with special needs and mental health difficulties.

1921-1923 Worked as local cultural official in Gomel.

1924 Met Luria at Second all-Russian Psycho-Neurological Congress in Leningrad. Lectures and articles on blind-deaf children. Travelled to London.

1925 *The Psychology of Art* (written).

1926 Founded laboratory for the study of Defectology. Educational Psychology (published).

1926-1931 Cultural Revolution in Russia.

1927 *The Historical Meaning of the Crisis in Psychology.*

1929 Establishment of Experimental Institute of Defectology.

1930 *The Socialist Alternative of Man* (written).

1930-35 *Mind and Society* (Published in US in 1978).

1931-33 Publication of articles on play and imagination.

1934 Vygotsky died of tuberculosis.

1934 *Thought and Language* (Published in US in 1962).

Lev Vygotsky was highly productive, writing hundreds of lectures and articles. The above list mentions a few of these. Many of Vygotsky's writings can be found in the Lev Vygotsky Archive at https://www.marxists.org/archive/vygotsky/

Glossary

These brief explanations of Vygotskian concepts are better understood in the context of his theory.

Affect/Affective This concept is used to refer to the emotional impact on a child/person.

Cognition Thinking and learning.

Concept An abstract idea that occurs in speech or thought

> **Everyday or Spontaneous** These are the concepts that are learnt through everyday life experiences and interaction. They are therefore learnt "bottom-up".

> **Scientific or Academic** These are the concepts specifically taught in school, because they are not picked up in daily interactions. They tend to be those that relate to schooling. They are therefore taught "top-down". Once learnt they act like spontaneous concepts, helping the learner to make sense of new, related concepts.

> **Protoconcept** The process of learning concepts is a gradual one. In the very early stages we have a rough idea of what a new concept means.

> **Pseudoconcept** As we mature or as adults become familiar with a new concept, we try it out, but not with a fully-fledged understanding of the true concept.

Commodity Fetishism A term used by Karl Marx in *A Contribution to a Critique of Political Economy*, to describe the way in which capitalism conceals the input of labour in the value of a product, attempting to make us believe that social relationships are in some way ruled by physical things, particularly in terms of their value.

Concretisation The process of embedding new concepts, making them real concepts.

Constructivism Based on the Piagetian notion that individual learners construct knowledge according to their previous knowledge, experiences and understandings. In Vygotskian terms, children develop through their learning experiences which take place between people and over time and in particular social/cultural settings.

Cultural Historical Psychology Based on Marxist dialectical materialism (see below), a psychological theory that shows the impact of social experiences over time on people's thinking or consciousness.

Cultural Mediation Through the use of social interactions, language, technology, tools, etc, a child comes to think and learn according to the traditions and meanings in her culture.

Defectology The study of principles and characteristics of education and development of children with physical and mental "impairments".

Dialectical Materialism A Marxist theory showing how our consciousness is a result of our material experiences over time. As Marx said in *A Contribution to the Critique of Political Economy* it is "social being" that determines consciousness.

Disontogenesis Where the development of the individual

becomes distorted, particularly through an unfavourable social environment.

Egocentric Speech The private, but verbalised speech of, particularly, young children used in the process of development – thinking aloud. This form of speech may not make sense to the outsider.

Inner or Internal Speech An internalised form of speech, used in thinking and in the process of transforming thought into language and language into thought.

Internalisation The process of understanding knowledge and actions through observations, social interactions and the use of tools and language. It is therefore the process of the development of higher mental functions.

Mental Functions

> **Higher Mental Functions** Conscious, deliberate thought processes that have been developed through social interactions. They differentiate humans from animals who do not have higher mental functions.

> **Lower Mental Functions** Thought processes that are not pre-meditated, usually reflex responses. They are similar to those of animals.

Paedology A dialectical study of the psychological and physical development of children.

Pedagogy Theory and practice of teaching.

Ontogenesis The development of an individual or an individual's trait.

Pioneer Programme Started by the Russian Communist Party in 1922, similar to the Scout Movement, for 9 to 15 year olds, to encourage social co-operation through volunteering work, sports and summer camps.

Phylogenesis The development of the species.

Pogrom State-backed massacre of people of a specific religious or ethnic group. Usually refers to the murder of Jews in Russia or Germany.

Reflexology Based on the stimulus-response theories of Pavlov, who believed that learning was a conditioned response (rather than social and cognitive process; mediated through language or other tools).

Scaffolding The temporary provision of instructional support by a more competent peer or adult, facilitating the internalisation of new knowledge.

Semiosis Where a sign, such as a word or image, represents a meaning.

Verbal Thought Thinking in words. This is in a different linguistic structure to speaking aloud.

Zone of Proximal Development The potential that a person has for learning in collaboration with others. This shows what a person can do with appropriate scaffolding, and shows the premature concepts that are already formed which are developed or "actualised" through purposeful interaction with another more knowledgable person.

Vygotsky's Blocks

Measurements

If you would like to make a set of Vygotsky's blocks here are the details and measurements:

mur

Tall and thin	Height of all 30mm	
Hexagon	all sides 14 mm	white
Cuboid	24 mm sides	yellow
Circle	27 mm diameter ,	one blue, one white
Triangle	sides 31 x 33 x 29mm	red

lag

Tall and fat	Height of all 30mm	
Trapezium	40 x 30 x 40 x 48 mm	yellow
Cuboid	38 mm sides	one blue, one red
Circle	52 mm diameter	red
Triangle	all sides 49mm	green

bik

Short and fat	Height of all 20mm	
Trapezium	38 x 26 x 38 x 46 mm	one red, one green
Cube	40 mm length, 38mm wide	green
Circle	55 mm diameter	blue
Semi-circle	68mm diameter	yellow
Triangle	all sides 49mm	white

cev

Short and thin	Height of all 20mm	
Hexagon	all sides 15 mm	white
Trapezium	26 x 18 x 26 x 35 mm	red
Circle	36 mm diameter	yellow
Semi-circle	40 diameter	green
Triangle	sides 38 x 38 x 40 mm	one yellow, one blue

Bibliography

Au, W. (2007) 'Vygotsky and Lenin on Learning: The Parallel Structures of Individual and Social Development' in *Science and Society,* Vol71. No.8 July 2007 273-298. http://lchc.ucsd.edu/MCA/Paper/AuVygotskyandLenin.pdf

BBC (1990) *The Butterflies of Zagorsk.* The story of the children at the deaf-blind school in Zagorsk, 40 miles North of Moscow, http://lchc.ucsd.edu/Movies/Butterflies_of_Zagorsk.mp4

Blonskii, P.P. (1964) I*zbrannye psikhologicheskie proizvedeniia* (*Selected Psychological Works*). Moscow: Prosveshchenie.

Bruner, J.S. (1985) 'Vygotsky: A Historical and Conceptual Perspective' in Wertsch, J.V. (ed.) *Culture Communication and Cognition: Vygotskyan Perspectives.* Cambridge: Cambridge University Press, pp.21-34.

Bruner, J. & Haste, H. (1987) *Making Sense.* London:Methuen

Cole, M. Levitin,K. & Luria.A. (2006) *The Autobiography of Alexander Luria. A Dialogue in the Making of Mind,* New Jersey: Lawrence Erlbaum

Daniels, H., Cole, M . & Wertsch, J. (eds.) (2007) *The Cambridge University Companion to Vygotsky.* Cambridge: Cambridge University Press

Fernández, M., Wegerif, R., Mercer, N., & Rojas-Drummond, S. (2002) 'Re-conceptualizing "scaffolding" and the zone of proximal development in the context of symmetrical collaborative learning' in *Journal of Classroom Interaction,* 36(2/1), pp. 40-54.

Freud, S. (1920, 2010) *Beyond the Pleasure Principle.* South Carolina: Createspace Independent Publishing Platform

John-Steiner, V. (2007) 'Vygotsky on Thinking and Speaking' in Daniels, H., Cole, M. & Wertsch, J.(eds.) (2007) *The Cambridge University Companion to Vygotsky.* Cambridge: Cambridge University Press.

Kellogg, D. & Veresov, N. (translators) (2019) *L.S. Vygotsky's Pedological Works,* Singapore: Springer.

Kotik-Friedgut, B. & Friedgut, T. (2008) 'A Man of His Country and Time: Jewish influences on Lev Semionovich Vygotsky's world view' in *History of Psychology,* Vol.11, No 1, pp.15-39.

Kozulin, A. & Gindis, B. (2007) 'Sociocultural Theory and Education of Children' in Daniels, et al *The Cambridge University Companion to Vygotsky.* Cambridge: Cambridge University Press pp. 332-362.

Lave, J. & Wenger, E. (1991) *Situated Learning: Legitimate Peripheral Participation* Cambridge: Cambridge University Press.

Lenin, V.I. (1902) *What is to be Done?* https://www.marxists.org/archive/lenin/works/1901/witbd/

Luria, A. (1935) 'Obituary for Lev Vygotsky', in *Character and Personality, An International Psychological Quarterly,* Volume III, No. 3, London.

Marx, K. (1857-58) *Grundrisse: Foundations of the Critique of Political Economy (Rough Draft).* Harmondsworth: Penguin, 1973 (First published in 1939 in German.)

Marx, K. (1867, 1961) *Capital, Volume 1.* London: Lawrence & Wishart

Marx, K (1970) *A Contribution to the Critique of Political Economy*. London: Lawrence and Wishart.

Marx ,K and Engels, F. (1974) *The German Ideology* London: Lawrence and Wishart.

Mercer, N. (2000) *Words and Minds: how we use language to think together*. London: Routledge.

Piaget, J. (1932) *The Moral Judgement of the Child,* Harcourt, Brace.

Piaget, J. (1962) Comments on Vygotsky's critical remarks concerning *The Language and Thought of the Child*, and *Judgment and Reasoning in the Child.* translated from the French by Dr. Anne Parsons; the translation was revised and edited by E. Hanfmann and G. Vakar; The MIT Press. http://www.marxists.org/archive/vygotsky/works/comment/piaget.htm

Peter Smagorinsky (2017) "Deconflating the ZPD and instructional scaffolding: Retranslating and reconceiving the zone of proximal development as the zone of next development" in *Learning, Culture and Social Interaction,* Elsevier Ltd. http://www.petersmagorinsky.net/About/PDF/LCSI/LCSI_2018.pdf

Tolstoy, L.N. (1964)"Komu u kogo uchit'sia pisat', krest'ianskim pebiatam u nas ili nam u krest'ianskikh rebiat?" (Who should be learning to write from whom, peasant children from us or us from peasant children?). In L.N. Tolstoi, *Sobranie sochinenii,* T. 15 (L.N. Tolstoy. *Collected Works.* Vol. 15). Moscow, 1964.

Trotsky, L. (2005) *Literature and Revolution* Chicago: Haymarket.
Van de Veer, R. (2007) *Lev Vygotsky* King's Lynn: Continuum
Van der Veer, R. (2007) 'Vygotsky in Context, 1900-1935' in Daniels, H., Cole, M. & Wertsch, J. (eds.) (2007) *The Cambridge*

University Companion to Vygotsky, Cambridge: Cambridge University Press. pp. 21-49.

Van der Veer, R. & Valsiner, J. (1991) *Understanding Vygotsky: a quest for synthesis*, Cambridge, MA, Oxford: Blackwell.

Van der Veer, R. & Valsiner, J. (1994) *The Vygotsky Reader*, Cambridge, MA, Oxford: Blackwell.

Van der Veer R. & Zavershneva, E (2011) 'To Moscow with Love: Partial Reconstruction of Vygotsky's Trip to London' in *Integrative Psychological Behavioural Science 45:4* (December 2011) pp458–474.

Volosinov, V. N. (1973) *Marxism and the Philosophy of Language*, Cambridge, Massachusetts: Harvard University Press.

Vygotsky, L.S. (1925). 'Consciousness as a problem in the psychology of behaviour' in *Soviet Psychology*, 17, pp.3–35. English translation by Nikolai Veresov. https://www.marxists.org/archive/vygotsky/works/1925/consciousness.htm

Vygotsky, L.S. (1926, 1997): *Educational Psychology*. N.W. Boca Ranton, Florida: CRC Press LLC.

Vygotsky, L.S. (1927, 1987) 'The Historical Meaning of the Crisis in Psychology: A Methodological Investigation' in the *Collected Works of Vygotsky*, 1987. New York and London: Plenum Press http://www.marxists.org/archive/vygotsky/works/crisis/index.htm_

Vygotsky, L.S. (1929) 'The Problem of the Cultural Development of the Child' in *The Pedagogical Seminary & Journal of Genetic Psychology*, 36, pp.415-32.

Vygotsky, L.S. (1930a) 'The Socialist Alternative of Man',

translated in R. Van der Veer & J. Valsiner (1994) *The Vygotsky Reader*, Oxford: Blackwell, pp.175-183.

Vygotsky, L.S. (1930b, 2004) 'Imagination and Creativity in Childhood' in *Journal of Russian and East European Psychology,* vol. 42, no. 1, (January–February 2004), pp. 7–97.

Vygotsky L.S. (1930c) *The Instrumental Method in Psychology.* Text of a talk given in 1930 at the Krupskaya Academy of Communist Education. https://www.marxists.org/archive/vygotsky/works/1930/instrumental.htm.

Vygotsky L.S. (1931) 'Imagination and Creativity in the Adolescent" *Soviet Psychology* 29,1 pp.73-88.

Vygotsky, L.S. (1933, 1967). 'Play and Its Role in the Mental Development of the Child', *Soviet Psychology* 5:6–18. Originally a lecture at Leningrad Pedagogical Institute https://www.marxists.org/archive/vygotsky/works/1933/play.htm

Vygotsky, L.S. (1962, 1986) *Thought and Language.* Cambridge, Massachusetts: MIT Press. (Original work published 1934).

Vygotsky, L.S. (1971) *The Psychology of Art.* Cambridge Mass:The MIT Press (Written in 1925 and originally published in the 1930's in Moscow).

Vygotsky, L.S. (1978): *Mind and Society: The Development of Higher Psychological Processes.* (eds. Michael Cole, Vera John-Steiner, Sylvia Scribner & Ellen Souberman, Eds.). Cambridge, MA: Harvard University Press.

Vygotsky, L.S. (1981): 'The Genesis of Higher Mental Functions' in J. V. Wertsch, (ed.) *The Concept of Activity in Soviet Psychology.* Armonk, N.Y.: M. E. Sharpe.

Vygotsky, L.S. (1987) *The Collected Works of L. S. Vygotsky. Volume 1: Problems of General Psychology,* Rieber, R.W. & and Carton, A.S. (eds.) New York: Plenum Press.

Vygotsky, L.S. (1993) *The Collected Works of L.S. Vygotsky. Volume 2: The Fundamentals of Defectology (Abnormal Psychology and Learning Disabilities)* Rieber, R.W. & and Carton, A.S. (eds.) New York: Plenum Press.

Vygotsky, L.S. (1997)*: The Collected Works of L. S. Vygotsky. Volume 3: The Problems of the Theory and History of Psychology (Cognition and Language: A Series in Psycholinguistics).*) R. W. Rieber and J.Wollock (eds.). New York: Plenum Press.

Vygotsky, L.S. (1997)*: The Collected Works of L. S. Vygotsky. Volume 4: The History of the Development of Higher Mental Functions* R. W. Rieber (ed.) New York: Plenum Press.

Vygotsky, L.S. (1998)*: The Collected Works of L. S. Vygotsky. Volume 5: Child Psychology Development of Higher Mental Functions* R. W. Rieber, (ed.) New York: Plenum Press.

Vygotsky, L.S. & Luria, A. (1930, 1993). *Studies on the history of behaviour. Ape, primitive, and child.* Hillsdale, NJ: Erlbaum.

Vygotsky, L.S. & Luria, A. (1939, 1994) 'Tool and symbol in child development' in Van der Veer, R. & Valsiner, J. (1994) *The Vygotsky Reader,* Cambridge, MA, Oxford: Blackwell pp.99-174. Vygodskaya, G.L. (1995) 'His Life'. *School Psychology International,* Vol.16, #2, pp.105-116. http://web.archive.org/web/20010430104821/www.j51.com/~tatyana/his_life.htm

Walkerdine, V. (1982) 'From Context to Text: a psychosemiotic approach to abstract thought' in M. Beveridge (ed.) *Children Thinking Through Language,* London: Arnold.

Wertsch, J. V. (ed.) (1985) *Culture Communication and Cognition: Vygotskyan perspectives.* Cambridge: Cambridge University Press

Wey, S. (2006) 'Working in The Zone — A social ecological framework for dementia rehab' in Woolham, J (ed) *Assistive Technology in Dementia Care*, Ch. 8. London: Hawker Publications

Wood, D.J., Bruner, J.S. & Ross, G. (1976) 'The role of tutoring in problem solving', *Journal of Child Psychiatry and Psychology,* 17(2), pp.89-100.

Yasnitsky, A. (2012) 'Lev Vygotsky: Philologist and defectologist, a sociointellectual biography' in W. E. Pickren, D. A. Dewsbury, & M. Wertheimer (eds.) *Portraits of Pioneers in Developmental Psychology,* New York, NY, US: Psychology Press., pp.109-133.

Yasnitsky, A. & Van der Veer, R. (eds.) (2016) *Revisionist Revolution in Vygotsky Studies* Hove: Routledge.

Zavershneva, E. & Van der Veer, R. (2018a) *Vygotsky's Notebooks—A selection,* Singapore: Springer

Zavershneva, E. & Van der Veer, R. (2018b) "Not by bread alone: Lev Vygotsky's Jewish writings" in *History of the Human Sciences*, 31(1) pp.36–55.

Notes

1   A note on language: Much of Vygotsky's work was in the field of Special Educational Needs, which in his day in Russia was known as Defectology. This is not a negative term, as we might suppose. Similarly, the terms "retarded" referred to some children with learning difficulties. There is a glossary at the end of the book which helps explain in more detail some of the new and complex concepts used.

2   Zavershneva and Van der Veer, 2018a.

3   This theory recognises the potential that we have for learning. We do not have a fixed level of understanding, as tests imply, but have a zone, dependent on our previous knowledge and experiences. See Chapter 6 for a detailed analysis of this interactional theory of how people learn new concepts.

4   These notebooks, edited by Zavershneva and Van der Veer, will hereafter referred to as *Vygotsky's Notebooks*

5   The *1936* Party *Decree on Paedological Distortions* banned all work, publications and study, related to pedagogy and psychology other than that produced by the State.

6   Vygotsky pointed out in his Preface to *Educational Psychology* that he was using the 'old terminology' in his analysis, since the new scientific language had not yet been established.

7   The Marxist Social Democratic Movement was the forerunner of the Bolshevik and Menshevik parties.

8   *Untold Stories* on the Yadvashem website details the Jewish history of Gomel.

9   Zavershneva and Van der Veer, 2018b.

10   For further information on the impact of Judaism on Vygotsky's life see Vygotsky's early writings in the *Notebooks*, 2018 and Kotik-Friedgut and Friedgut, 2008.

11   *Vygotsky's Notebooks*, p.40

12   *Golus*, a Yiddish term, refers to the dispersal of Jews throughout the diaspora (i.e. not Israel).

13   *Vygotsky's Notebooks* p.44.

14   As a lawyer he would have been permitted to live and work outside the confines of the Jewish settlements.

15   Cited by his daughter, Gita Vygodskaya, 1995.

16   Cited by Gita Vygodskaya, 1995.

17   This apprenticeship pedagogical model was later developed by Lave and Wenger in their work on *Communities of Practice* and *Situated Learning.*

18   *Educational Psychology*, p.345.

19   Van der Veer & Valsiner, 1991 p.56.

20   Van der Veer, 2007

21   Van der Veer & Valsiner, 1994:27-45

22   Marx, K. and Engels, F. 1974, p.47.

23   Published in 1993.

24   Van der Veer and Valsiner, 1994, pp.19-25.

25   *Vygotsky's Notebooks* pp.57- 70.

26   *Vygotsky's Notebooks*, p.62-3.

27   *Vygotsky's Notebooks*, p.64.

28   In Van der Veer, R. & Zavershneva, 2011, p.469.

29   in Van der Veer and Valsiner, 1991, p.13.

30   in Van der Veer and Valsiner, 1991, p.13.

31   Published in the USA in 1978.

32   In Vygotsky, 1987.

33   Trotsky, 1924/2005 pp.206-207.

34   Cited in Van der Veer & Valsiner, 1991, p.55.

35   Paedology differs from pedagogy - paedology is a sociocognitive study of children's development and the adaptation of teaching methods to that development, whereas pedagogy is the theory and practice of teaching

36   *Vygotsky's Notebooks*, p118.

37   Van der Veer and Valsiner, 1991.

38   Kellogg and Veresov, p.V.

39   Yasnitsky and Van der Veer, 2016.

40   See Van der Veer, 2007.

41   Vygotsky, 1926, 1997 p.232.

42   Van der Veer & Valsiner 1991, p.14.

43   Yasnistky & Van der Veer 2016, p.43.

44   Van der Veer, 2007,pp. 27 - 9

45   From *Historical Meaning of the Crisis in Psychology*, 1927 quoted in Wertsch, 1985, p.6.

46   Marx, 1961, p.178

47   Vygotsky 1925, 2000.

48   *Vygotsky's Notebooks*, p.74.

49   *Vygotsky's Notebooks*, p.74.

50   *Vygotsky's Notebooks*, p.76.

51 Vygotsky, 1930c.
52 Marx, 1890, 1981, p.192.
53 Vygotsky 1978, p.40.
54 Marx and Engels, 1974 p.51.
55 This work is now more generally translated as *Thinking and Speech* to denote the process of thinking.
56 Vygotsky, 1978, p.89.
57 The blocks were originally developed by the German psychologist Narziss Ach, working on word associations.
58 Vygotsky, 1986, pp.103-4.
59 Vygotsky, 1986, p.124
60 Vygotsky, 1986, p.193.
61 Vygotsky, 1986, p.193.
62 Vygotsky, 1986, pp.193-194.
63 Vygotsky, 1986, p.148. This point has often been overlooked, especially by educationalists who erroneously draw on Vygotsky to argue for informal activity-based learning, without teacher intervention. These people fail to understand the varied learning processes involved in the educational context and the significance of academic concepts. This issue will be further addressed in the educational pedagogical section below.
64 Au, 2007
65 Lenin, 1901.
66 The zone of proximal development will be explored further in the next section.
67 Vygotsky, 1978, p.57.
68 Vygotsky, 1978, p.73
69 Vygotsky, 1986, p. 86.
70 Vygotsky, L. S. & Luria, A. (1939, 1994), p.109.
71 Vygotsky, 1986, p.250.
72 John-Steiner, 2007, pp.141-2.
73 Vygotsky, 1986, pp.94-95.
74 Vygotsky, 1978, p.88.
75 Bruner, in Wertsch 1985, pp. 24-5.
76 Vygotsky, 1978, p.86.
77 Vygotsky 1986, p.188.
78 Mercer, 2000 and in Fernández, et al 2002, p.55
79 Vygotsky, 1978, p.90.
80 Vygotsky, 1926, 1997, p.58
81 Vygotsky, 1997, p.212.
82 Vygotsky, 1978, p.89.
83 Vygotsky, 1998, p.205.
84 See Kozulin and Gindis in Daniels, et al. pp.352-362.
85 Wey, 2006.
86 Bruner and Haste, 1987, p.1.
87 Vygotsky, 1931, 2004 p.7.
88 Vygotsky, 1933, 1967. It is also published in *Mind and Society*. This book refers to the online version available at https://www.marxists.org/archive/vygotsky
89 Vygotsky, 1931 2004.
90 Vygotsky, 1931, 2004, p.15.
91 Vygotsky, 1931, 2004, p. 9.
92 Vygotsky, 1931, 2004, p.55.
93 Vygotsky, 2004, p.19
94 Vygotsky, 1931, p.26.
95 Vygotsky, 1931, p.37.
96 Vygotsky, 1931 p. 41.
97 Vygotsky, L.S. 1933, 1967.
98 *Vygotsky's Notebooks*, p.459, 1933/4
99 Marx, 1976, p. 614
100 Interestingly, the chapter in *Mind and Society*, which is taken from this lecture, completely misses these crucial points.
101 Vygotsky, 1933
102 Vygotsky, 1933
103 Previously, throughout his research in psychology, Vygotsky had critiqued Piaget for not acknowledging the role of society and culture in the cognitive development of the child. However, later, Piaget began to incorporate a social dimension into his analysis.
104 Vygotsky drew on the work of his old hero Spinoza. In Part III of his *Ethics*, Spinoza had said that an affect can be overcome, become a stronger affect, a passion. In other words where the child is emotionally affected, this enjoyment can counteract or reinforce the rule-keeping in a game.
105 Vygotsky, 1933
106 Vygotsky, 1931, 2004, pp. 5-6
107 Vygotsky, 1933
108 Vygotsky, 1933
109 Vygotsky, 1931, 2004, p.71.
110 Vygotsky,1978, p.106
111 Vygotsky, 1978, p.107
112 Vygotsky, 1978, p.115
113 Vygotsky, 1978, pp115-6
114 Vygotsky, 1931, 2004.
115 He had grown up in an environment steeped in literature.
116 Vygotsky 1931, 2004, p.45.
117 Tolstoy, 1964.
118 Vygotsky, 1931, 2004, p.46
119 Vygotsky, 1931, 2004, p.47.
120 Vygotsky, 1931, 2004 p.45.
121 Vygotsky, 1931, 2004, p. 53.
122 Vygotsky, 1931. 2004 p.69.
123 Vygotsky, 1931, 2004 p.51.
124 Vygotsky, 1931, 2004 pp.87-88!
125 Vygotsky, 1993, p.16.
126 A selection of these writings is published

in a collection, *The Fundamentals of Defectology,* 1993 and an article in *The Vygotsky Reader. Vygotsky's Notebooks* also include his notes of children with emotional disturbance.

127 Vygotsky, 1929, 1993 pp. 20-51.

128 Vygotsky, 1929, 1993, pp.50-51.

129 Vygotsky, 1929, 1993, p. 29.

130 Vygotsky, 1924, 1993, p.92.

131 Vygotsky, 1993 p.76.

132 Vygotsky, 1993, p.57.

133 Vygotsky, 1993, pp.62-3.

134 Vygotsky, 1993, pp.63.

135 Vygotsky, 1993, p.14.

136 In Van der Veer & Valsiner (eds) 1994, p.19 – 26.

137 In Van der Veer & Valsiner (eds) 1994, p.20.

138 In Van der Veer and Valsiner, 1994, p.21.

139 In Van der Veer and Valsiner, 1994, p.24

140 In Van der Veer and Valsiner. 1994, p.22.

141 In Van der Veer and Valsiner. 1994, p.23.

142 In Van der Veer & Valsiner, 1994, p.24.

143 BBC, *The Butterflies of Zagorsk* (first broadcast in 1990) The story of the children at the deaf-blind school in Zagorsk, 40 miles North of Moscow, can be seen on http://lchc.ucsd.edu/Movies/Butterflies_of_Zagorsk.mp4 and in the BFI Library

144 Vygotsky's *Notebooks* pp. 437-458.

145 Vygotsky's *Notebooks* pp. 447.

146 Vygotsky, 1993p.64.

147 Vygotsky,1978, p.89.

148 Vygotsky, 1993 p.84.

149 Vygotsky, 1993 p.83.

150 Marx , 1867, 1961, p.483.

151 Vygotsky in Van der Veer and Valsiner, 1994, p.25.

152 Vygotsky 1993, p.45.

153 Vygotsky, 1993 p.83.

154 Vygotsky, 1926, 1997, p. 348.

155 Vygotsky, 1931, p.9